shalom
MY FRIENDS

FOR THE KIREIDERS
WHO WORKED IN SHALOM
TO PRESENT SHALOM

THANK-YOU

BAPTIST ASSEMBLY 1988

Colin Marchant

shalom
MY FRIENDS
BUILDING GOD'S KINGDOM TOGETHER

Colin Marchant

Marshall Pickering

Acknowledgements

The author would like to acknowledge use of short extracts from the works of the authors listed in the References section of this book, and to Weidenfeld and Nicolson for use of material from Margaret Drabble's *Jerusalem the Golden*.

Marshall Morgan and Scott
Marshall Pickering
3 Beggarwood Lane, Basingstoke, Hants RG23 7LP, UK

Copyright © 1988 Colin Marchant
First published in 1988 by Marshall Morgan and Scott Publications Ltd
Part of the Marshall Pickering Holdings Group
A subsidiary of the Zondervan Corporation

ISBN: 0 551 01615 9

Text set in Baskerville by Brian Robinson, Buckingham
Printed in Great Britain by Richard Clay Ltd, Bungay, Suffolk

Contents

Foreword   ix

1 Begin Here   1

   The Word
   Reasons and Readers
   Purpose and Shape
   The Journey

2 Greetings!   9

   Contemporary Echoes
   Rooted in the Old Testament
   Embodied in Jesus
   Shalom Says it All

3 The One Dream   17

   The Dream is Real
   Becomes a Prayer
   Many Levels
   Appears in Many Guises
   Holds Together Past and Future
   Living Towards a Vision

4 The Double Reality   28

   Shalom is Positive
   The Negative Opposition
   The Conflict in the Bible
   The Battle Today

5 The Gift of God   37

   The Gift as Blessing
   Bringing Prosperity and Reward
   Holding Together Personal and Corporate
   Always Embodied and Earthed
   Penetrating All

6 Rooted In Us   48

   Earthed in Response
   The Covenant
   Deep-seated in People
   Carried in Task
   Ingrained in Place

7 Make It Personal   61

   Personal Well-being
   At All Levels
   In Many Ways
   Overcoming the Barriers
   Salvation – Being Made Whole
   The Shalom Life Style

8 For Sharing   80

   The Central Theme
   In Relationships
   In Friendship
   In Society
   Becoming Peacemakers
   The Shalom Agenda
   Signs of Hope

9 To Be Universal   96

   Within the Nation
   Between Nations
   The Whole Earth

10 Foundations   109

    The Necessity
    False Foundations
    Real Foundations
    Righteousness and Justice

11 Continuation   118

    Keeping the Covenant
    Consequences:
        Personal Life Style
        In the Shalom Community
        In the Wider World

12 Consummation   136

    Towards the Goal
    Personal Wholeness
    Universal Shalom
    Living in the In-Between

13 Farewell   144

    Profoundly Personal
    Wholeness and Healing Be Yours

14 A Biblical Quarry   150

15 Contemporary Workshop   170

    References   176

Foreword

The title of the book spells out the theme – this is an exploration and application of one word, shalom. This powerful Biblical word speaks to our time and to our needs. It has spoken to me within the inner city context and I have taken it as the theme for my time as President of the Baptist Union for 1988/89.

The drawing on the front cover gives a backcloth. The symbol of the cross and the circle is ancient in origin, theological in meaning and contemporary in usage.

The cross within a ring was an Egyptian hieroglyphic for a city from 1800 BC – indicating the cross-roads of communication surrounded by a developing community. But the sign is also the Celtic or Iona Cross where the rising sun of the resurrection frames the message of the crucifixion.

It is now a contemporary logo for the Evangelical Coalition of Urban Mission which draws together men and women engaged in training for the work of evangelism, those wrestling with racism, youth workers reaching out to frontier young people and those thinking their way through urban issues.

So in itself the sign holds together time – 1800 BC, BC/AD and the 1980s; the urban – stressing hurt and healing, communications and community; and the Gospel – cross and resurrection, wholeness and unity.

That is why the artist has the encircling city wall, the four segments covering the entire span of human experience and the linking cross covering all.

Behind, and sometimes within, the book, stand a crowd of men and women who mean more to me than I can ever say. They are the shalom people who carry within themselves the hope and healing of our society. Some have provided the quotations about shalom, many more have visibly shown the fruit of shalom.

I gratefully acknowledge the help of all those who by picture, words, or life have assisted in the birth of this book.

Aston Charities, who employ me, gave space and freedom, the Baptist Congregation to which I belong in East London have kept alive thought and action, and my own family have sustained and encouraged me.

Four women (as always) have been involved in the details. Christine Whitell of Marshalls has kept me at it, Pat Deal and Pat Wiggins typed their way through my appalling handwriting and Judith, my wife and friend, has embodied shalom.

If you really want to use this book take it steadily and apply it carefully. Let it be more like a lozenge you suck slowly than a drink you gulp hastily! Take a chapter at a time, for each explores one aspect of shalom. Think it through. Use the Bible Quarry for detailed work. Since I believe that few people ever bother to look up Biblical references I have allowed the Bible to speak for itself.

If you want to team up with others or pursue your own concerns you can follow through on the resource list.

Colin Marchant
April 1988

Begin Here

In the beginning was the Word.   John 1:1 (AV)

Shalom.

The Word

Shalom.

One Word.

I want to introduce you to the word and the theme. Shalom, of course, is a Bible word. It occurs 250 times in the Hebrew Bible, the Old Testament, and 90 times in the New Testament (in its Greek translation, *eirene*).

Shalom is a contemporary word. It speaks today to our lifestyle, our relationships, and our attitudes.

Because it is such a comprehensive, rich and earthy word it is hard to translate. Most people think shalom means peace – but it is much more. It has to do with well-being and wholeness; it is both personal and social; it is known in time and fulfilled in eternity; it is the purpose of God and the dream of the human race.

You can begin to think about it by looking at the circles of meaning and messages that flow from shalom . . .

PRESENCE OF GOD
BLESSING
GREETING
PRAYER

WHOLE
INTACT
SOUND
BODILY HEALTH

PERFECTION
FREE FROM FAULT
WELL BEING
WELFARE

GIFT OF GOD
SHALOM
COVENANT

TRUST
SLEEP
DEATH
CONSUMMATION

UNITY
FRIENDS
HARMONY
RIGHT RELATIONS

PEACE
DOING RIGHT
JUSTICE
SALVATION

Reasons and Readers

But why a book on shalom? I intended to write about urban
spirituality. I sketched out an outline, gathered together the
material, set out my notes – but all the time I kept coming
back to this one word! There are four strong reasons behind
this book.

The first reason is that *shalom speaks from, and to, the urban
realities*. I am an urban Christian. All my life has been spent
in cities or large towns – beginning in the suburbs of
London, working on a housing estate in Birmingham, living
in the changing town of Luton and settling in the inner city
scene of East London. For over 20 years I have lived and
worked in the London Borough of Newham in a variety of
roles; within the family – husband, father and grandfather;
within one Baptist Church – pastor, team leader, deacon
and member. We have lived in a church manse, a residential
community centre and our own home. Here we have raised
a family, joined in community life and wrestled with the way
Christian faith speaks (or does not speak) to an industrial
area. We have shared in the development of urban networks

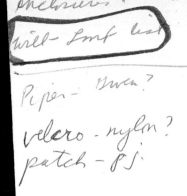

enclosures + mail
will send list

Piper - Gwen?

velcro - nylon?
patch - PJ.

ve been pushed back to the roots of
he only way and the only word that
lom. This is the message the inner
ie individual, the groups within the
ional setting. But this is also the
gations have to share with their
sters. It is a positive and powerful
reflected from, the urban areas.
at _shalom is a dream word_. It gathers
be, all that I pray for others, and
e. Shalom has to do with yearning
elf the over-all purpose of God and
is closely linked with the proclamation of the kingdom of
God. In this sense, it is both a present experience and a
future goal – it both is, but has yet to be. It calls us to live
towards a vision. Because of this, shalom is a key word:
opening doors, letting in the light, allowing in the fresh air
and encouraging movement. It provides access to new
horizons and necessary resources – we all need both.

Thirdly, _shalom is a Bible word_. The word itself, and the
message it carries, runs through the whole of Scripture like a
place-name runs through a stick of seaside rock – appearing
wherever you break it. Shalom is used to describe the well-
being of the individual, it has to do with harmony in
relationships and is a pivotal word in the covenant between
God and his People. In the Psalms people sing about shalom
and pray for it; the prophets proclaim God's shalom; the
Gospels see shalom in Jesus and the Letters to the young
churches tell individuals and groups how to live in shalom.
In Scripture shalom is a diamond word: multifaceted,
reflecting light from many angles, immensely strong and of
great worth.

Finally, _shalom is an action word_. It is dynamic and not
static, like the well-ordered business of beehive or anthill. It
is communal with a stress on relationships. It is outward in
its direction towards the created world, rather than an
interior feeling. It is positive, working for the presence of
good rather than being the mere absence of disturbance. It is

radical, for the emergence of shalom (whether it be wholeness for the world, the church, or the individual) requires fundamental changes in our values, presuppositions and perceptions. Shalom is both being and doing.

Those are the reasons for this book. A profound conviction that shalom is a deeply rooted but vividly contemporary word for the urban people; a recognition that shalom is a word of comprehensive vision; the fact that it is biblical through and through; and that it stimulates, undergirds and empowers action. In short, shalom is a theme for today. I hope it is a word for you.

The title of this book, *Shalom, My Friends* is the opening sentence of a chorus, but it also describes my target. Shalom is often translated in terms of friendship. I am, therefore, writing for and to my friends.

You are clustered under two umbrellas! One group are those of you who, in Bible terms, want to be 'the friends of God' – the shalom people. Whether you are engaged in urban mission or not, you are deeply concerned about the urban process, wrestling with biblical truth, yearning for the power of a comprehensive vision, and wanting action rather than debate.

The other group who are often in my mind, and beside me in much of my work, are my friends who are not card-carrying Christians. You, too, are searching for meaning and hope in the urban confusion and struggles. From political or humanitarian motive, you are involved and committed. Sometimes you feel desperately lonely and often you experience a great weariness. Shalom is the word for you.

All who read this book need to know that it was not written in the seclusion of a study or in the well-planned programme of the academic. This book was drawn up in a busy centre for caring and community in East London during a time of major personal change. During the final draft I changed my address and my job and moved into a new life pattern!

Change may be exciting and even creative but it is also disturbing and can even be bereavement. We have had to strive to keep shalom: Within us and around us the complexity and opportunity of urban mission has brought its own demands and delights.

Purpose and Shape

The purpose of this book can be summed up in one sentence – **To make shalom real**. Real in idea and earthing. Real for you, for me, and for all. Therefore I have set out to:

● Introduce you to the Bible themes and messages gathered together in shalom.

● Uncover the vision recorded in Scripture, embodied in Jesus (the shalom person), experienced by the first disciples and carried through to our own day.

● Break down the over-all harmony of shalom into the separate and distinctive notes. So each chapter focuses on one important strand within the complete picture.

● Link these insights to our contemporary situation – personal, corporate and national.

● Encourage you to work at the biblical material for yourself and to follow through on resources and ways ahead.

● Help all of us to be the shalom people following the shalom person bringing shalom to the whole of creation.

After this 'diving board' introduction we will plunge into a search for shalom. This section begins with a chapter on 'Greetings' (what do we really wish for others and ourselves?), goes on to 'The one dream' that grips and inspires us and ends with a look at 'The double reality' we all face in our human experience.

When we look more closely at the pattern of shalom we will see how it is a 'Gift of God' which must be 'Rooted in Us' – holding together God's initiative and our response. This is known at the individual, social and universal levels carried in the chapters 'Made Personal', 'For Sharing' and 'To be Universal'.

Under the process of shalom there will be a check on the 'Foundations' upon which we build, the struggles and joys in 'Continuation' and the final 'Consummation' of shalom for individuals, the church and the world.

The book will conclude with 'Farewell' which will draw out the prayers and hopes carried in shalom and sketch out an agenda for action.

Then for those who want to keep on working I have provided a 'Biblical Quarry' where you can dig more deeply and systematically and a 'Contemporary Workshop' which gathers together some resources and routes available to the shalom seeker.

The Journey

We are not the first to take this journey. Many have preceded us and others will follow. Our life in time is like a prolonged relay race with a continual 'passing of the baton' from one to the other.

The life accounts of a crowd of pilgrims are to be found in the Bible. I have obviously derived so much from the Scriptures. The Bible quotations (and the abbreviations of the books) are all taken from the Good News Bible (Today's English Version) which has a preface to remind us:

> The Bible is not simply great literature to be admired and revered; it is Good News for all people everywhere – a message both to be understood and to be applied in daily life.

The word shalom and its derivatives (whatever the English translation may be) are in a bold typeface in all the biblical quotations. Whenever you see the biblical references in bold print you will know the word shalom is being used.

All else is drawn from my own pilgrimage. I owe so much to the many I have walked with who have been shalom people. There is one man in particular who introduced me to shalom. Jim Punton was the Training Officer of the Frontier

Youth Trust and a biblical scholar. His untimely death removed a prophet who was both activist and thinker – but the message goes on.

Then there are three books whose titles and authors say so much about the issues and application of shalom.

● *Towards the Recovery of a Lost Bequest*[1] by Roger Dowley is the work of a solicitor who has chosen to live, with his wife Ruth, in inner London for all of his working life (and now into retirement) and he has written 'a layman's work-notes on the Bible Pattern for a Just Community'.

● *Living Toward a Vision*[2] by Walter Brueggemann is a shalom resource book from the United Church in the USA. Here are 'biblical reflections on shalom' written by a scholar who is a passionate seeker after social justice.

● *Shalom: The Bible's Word for Salvation, Justice, and Peace*[3] by Perry B. Yoder blends biblical theology with Third World exposure.

A quotation from each book will give you direction and impetus as you travel on. In a chapter titled 'Action in the Brickyard' Walter Brueggemann says:

> Shalom is such an abstract word in our ears that we need to find ways to make it concrete. The Bible never talks about shalom in an abstract or fuzzy way. It is always very specific and concrete . . . God's shalom is always embodied in such a way that people know it is happening in their historical experience.[4]

Arguing that shalom be at the centre of faith Perry Yoder writes:

> We should make a renewed effort to place shalom more centrally in our proclamation and struggle. Placing matters relating to peace on the outer edge of faith, making them an optional, individual matter of conscience, and reducing the meaning of peace to a passive avoidance of violence, have all skewed our understanding of both shalom and the central core of biblical faith.[5]

In urging us to grasp the full scope of shalom Roger Dowley points out:

In Christian tradition the English word 'peace' has been used mostly to mean 'inner peace' or 'peace with God'. The popularisation in recent years of the Hebrew word 'shalom' has opened the way to an understanding of the idea in a communal rather than private sense, particularly among those who are trying to recover the New Testament conception of koinonia-fellowship. Even here, however, the meaning can be limited to that of a comfortable sensation to be enjoyed, without any awareness of the principle that God's shalom is indivisible from justice. That if injustice is left unchallenged it will destroy shalom as inevitably as a potentially active volcano will one day overwhelm a green and fruitful countryside.[6]

There it is. I have introduced you to the word, given my reasons for writing this book, reached out to 'include you in', set out my purpose, sketched the shape of the book, and called you to begin a journey. Travel on!

Still sensing after some way of defining my lifestyle and beliefs, I went off to theological college, where in my first year, I met Jim Punton, the training and education officer for Britain's Frontier Youth Trust. My encounter with him was a memorable and life-changing one, and gave my discipleship fresh impetus. I first heard him talk about 'the gospel of shalom' at a chapel service. It was a disturbing, exhilarating and deeply moving experience. I sensed that here was the theological concept I had been grasping after intuitively. What's more Jim demonstrated that it came with an impeccable biblical pedigree.[7]

Bruce Dutton *Green Shoots in the Concrete*

Greetings!

Peace be with you.

Jesus to his disciples

At root shalom means 'well-being' with a strong emphasis on the material side. In meetings or letters well-being is wished for others, and in conversations we ask about their well-being.

Theological Dictionary of the New Testament[1]

Contemporary Echoes

Start with greetings. Most people do. Look at the signals of recognition. Listen to the way we greet each other. Eavesdrop down the street, in a bus, by a market stall . . . what do you hear?

There is the quick, almost perfunctory 'Good morning' or 'Good evening'. You'll hear the formal 'How do you do?'; the import from the USA 'Have a nice day' or the more usual 'How are you?' often lengthened and strengthened to 'How are you getting on?' More colloquial greetings are heard in 'Take care' or 'All the best' with the even more localised 'Wotcher' (what cheer?) and 'Best of luck'.

Hidden in these greetings is a message. Tucked away behind the well-worn words is a theme. All are concerned about the welfare or good health. The use of the word 'good' or the interested question are linked. Your friends are wanting the best for you. They are contemporary echoes of shalom. The greetings are (almost) a prayer.

Usually they are personalised. You are singled out in a crowd, named, addressed. And that means a relationship. The person who greets you knows you, in some sense appreciates (loves) you and is genuinely concerned about you as a person.

The outward forms of our greetings – the nod, the tip of a hat, the kiss on the cheek, the hallo, the wave – may have become superficial, careless or habitual but they are still the channels of concern.

Where we live there is a wide variety of greetings – not all of them polite! All around us people are using fingers or hands, eyes or lips, heads or arms to convey something to another. And almost all greetings have at their root a concern for the other's welfare.

Greetings do something. They are bridges for traffic – and this is usually two-way. A wave across a street gets a response. A shout arrests attention. A sentence is returned. An embrace is answered.

When the verbal and visual greetings are put together they are full of meaning. Two letters, OK, plus a 'thumbs up' sign say a lot. Through the windows of a passing car, over a crowded street, on the underground escalators the message comes over, 'OK?' – 'you all right?' 'everyone else OK?'

When we cannot see, hear or touch each other we send written greetings. Each year individuals receive birthday greetings that single them out, recall their uniqueness and carry affection. At Christmas everybody greets each other in a welter of family and friendship 'good wishes' conveyed through cards.

Greetings lift, encourage and identify. They are a public statement of friendship or a very personal expression of love. They are a check-up on shalom, even at the original level of material well-being or prosperity – wishing you well.

Rooted in the Old Testament

The Scriptures are full of greetings. In wide variety and astonishing number, human beings welcome each other – or are greeted by God. They wish for each other the experiences of well-being, wholeness, health and harmony which are wrapped up in the word shalom. That word is used in many greetings. The commonly used word is filled with a variety of meanings, ranging from that of simple friendship to a human-divine relationship.

In the Old Testament, greetings using shalom are used at many levels. There is the personal greeting from one individual to another; as in David's message to Nabal:

David sends you **greetings**, my friend, with his best wishes for you, your family, and all that is yours. (1 Sam 25:6)

Or the greeting from an individual to a group seen in the reassuring welcome back the King gave to those who had faltered and failed in the battle:

They came forward to meet David and his men, and David went up to them and **greeted** them warmly. (1 Sam 30:21)

But the ripples spread even more widely from individual to group, from nation to the world. In two Psalms there is the greeting, or the prayer for shalom, that reaches out to the whole nation in the closing words:

Peace be with Israel. (ending Pss 125 and 128)

Here these closing words end two short songs which are themselves shorthand summaries of a 'people' being in shalom.

And Darius the Mede, King of Babylon, takes the Hebrew shalom into his universal greetings:

Then King Darius wrote to the people of all nations, races, and languages on earth: **Greetings!** (Dan 6:25)

Embodied in Jesus

In the New Testament Jesus takes up and develops the idea of greeting. Having grown up aware of the custom of his own society of using greetings to convey the hope of shalom, he commands his disciples and followers to take shalom (a translation of the Greek *eirene*) wherever they go.

When the first 12 disciples are sent out on their mission they are told by Jesus to link their greeting with the hope of shalom. The drive towards human wholeness is seen in the command to heal every disease and sickness, to cast out evil spirits, to go to the lost and to bring the dead back to life.

> When you go into a house, say '**Peace** be with you'. If the people in that house welcome you, let your **greeting of peace** remain; but if they do not welcome you take back your **greeting**'. (Mt 10:12–13)

Later, the larger group of 72 are sent out by Jesus with the command that underlines and endorses the first charge:

> Whenever you go into a house, first say '**Peace** be with this house'. If a **peace-loving** man lives there, let your **greeting of peace** remain on him; if not take back your **greeting of peace**. (Lk 10:5–6)

The followers have grown in number, the command is linked with the news of the coming of the Kingdom and stress is laid on the judgement that follows rejection, but the central theme of shalom continues.

What the disciples carry in words, Jesus embodies in life. He is God's greeting. He is shalom. That message is illustrated within his ministry which in itself is a prolonged greeting to the forgotten, marginalised and damaged people. All that he is, says, and does is an incarnation of shalom.

His disciples only fully and finally understand this when the Easter greeting – '**Peace** be with you' is given to them:

> Then Jesus came and stood among them. '**Peace** be with you', he said. After saying this he showed them his hands and his side. The disciples were filled with joy at seeing the Lord. Jesus said to them again '**Peace** be with you'. As the Father sent me, so I send you. (Jn 20:19–21)

The greeting inaugurates a new era and the disciples are

sent out to the whole world to carry the shalom message in words and in life. Their fear is removed, disbelief is scattered, the continuing commission is given, and the enabling power of the Holy Spirit comes to the Church. For them Jesus is the shalom bearer, the giver of wholeness and the embodiment of healing.

Some, like Peter, preach it:

> You know the message he sent to the people of Israel, proclaiming the Good News of **peace** through Jesus Christ. (Acts 10:36)

Those who first received this greeting pass it on. Others underline it in the letters they wrote to each other. Right at the start, in letter after letter, like the words of Paul to the Christians in Rome:

> May God our Father and the Lord Jesus Christ give you grace and **peace**. (Rom 1:7)

Sometimes the greeting is personalised – as when Paul writes to the younger Chrsitian leader, Timothy:

> To Timothy, my true son in the faith: May God the Father and Christ Jesus our Lord give you grace, mercy, and **peace**. (1 Tim 1:2)

More often, the peace is sent to the group, the congregation:

> From Paul, Silas, and Timothy – to the people of the church in Thessalonica, who belong to God the Father and the Lord Jesus Christ. May grace and **peace** be yours. (1 Thes 1:1)

Whether the shalom greeting is personal or corporate there is a fulness and a wholeness about this Christian salutation. The writers wrestle to convey that wholeness, in the way they cluster truth, mercy and grace around the word peace; in the way they both open and end their letters with peace; and in the way the greeting is seen to be transmitted from the Father God through the Son Jesus to the believer:

May God the Father and Jesus Christ, the Father's Son, give us grace, mercy, and **peace**; may they be ours in truth and love. (2 Jn 3)

So from Genesis to Revelation the shalom greeting rings out. Whether it be the very human re-assurance the servant gives to Joseph's brother:

'Don't worry. **Don't be afraid.** (Gen 43:23)

Whether it be the dramatic and lyrical 'Greetings to the Seven Churches' in the last book of the Bible:

Grace and **peace** be yours from God, who is, who was, and who is to come . . . and from Jesus Christ, the faithful witness, the first to be raised from death and who is also the ruler of the kings of the world. He loves us, and by his death he has freed us from our sins and made us a kingdom of priests to serve his God and Father. To Jesus Christ be the glory and power for ever and ever. Amen. (Rev 1:4–6)

Shalom Says It All

Here is the purpose of God for each individual, all relationships, every nation and the entire creation. Echoes and hints of this message are conveyed in the human and divine greetings that are all around us. Watered down, covered over, weakened by time or lost in the language . . . it has not been obliterated or forgotten.

At the heart of Christian worship comes The Peace. In this custom, now rapidly spreading into all churches, believers greet each other verbally and physically before the bread and the wine.

Christ is our peace.
He has reconciled us to God in one body by the cross.
We meet in his name and share his peace.
We are the Body of Christ.

In the one Spirit we were all baptised into one body.
Let us then pursue all that makes for peace and builds up
our common life.
The peace of the Lord be always with you.
Let us offer one another a Sign of Peace.[2]

The use of the words, the embrace (not always easy for the
reserved English!) and the desire that this shalom should be
known to, and shared by, all are woven together in this
powerful act of symbolism. For me, the greeting has now
become indelibly that of the urban Christian. I do not know
how, or when, it started. I noticed the word shalom
appearing at the end of a letter instead of the more formal
'Yours faithfully'. Then it became verbal as the word,
accompanied by the raising of a hand in greeting, was
exchanged in the street. Finally, word and action fused into
the embrace used both inside and outside of worship and in
the gathering together of urban Christians.

It is, of course, a universal greeting. In 1986 I went to the
Chicago Urban Mission Conference. It opened in a huge
hotel auditorium with hundreds of Christians, previously
strangers to each other, breaking into song, whirling round
tables, linking arms and joining in the chorus 'Shalom, my
friends'.

Shalom, my friends,
God be with you
In all you do.
Shalom, Shalom.

Shalom, then, for me, is *the* greeting. It speaks to the inner
city dweller in the personal struggle for a complete and full
life, in the conflicting cultural and racial relationships and in
the sense of external pressures bearing down in oppression
and hurt. But it is God's greeting to all. To the individual we
meet on the train, write to in a letter, hear at the end of a
phone – or belong to in a family or friendship. For him or for
her – it is 'Shalom, my friend'.

To the diverse groups in whom we live, move and have

our being – peer groups, professional bodies, congregations, neighbourhood or national. For, and in, them all it is 'Shalom, my friends'. To the races from which we spring or the nations to which we belong – in the confusions, divisions and racisms. There it is to be 'Shalom, my friends'. To the whole earth, and even the universe. The greeting is visionary and comprehensive. All is to be one. Shalom to creation!

This is *the* greeting. God's shalom to his creation and to us all. It comes to us and, hopefully, through us. It is his vision and our dream.

A Definition of Shalom

Total harmony within the community. It is founded upon order and permeated by God's blessing, and makes it possible for man to develop and increase free and unhindered on every side.[3]

Encyclopaedia of Biblical Theology

The One Dream

> *Your sons and daughters will proclaim my message,*
> *your young men shall see visions, and your old men will*
> *have dreams.*
>
> Acts 2:17 quoting Joel 2:28

> *The central vision of world history in the Bible is that*
> *all of creation is one, every creature in community with*
> *every other, living in harmony and security toward the*
> *joy and well being of every other creature.* [1]
>
> Walter Brueggemann

The Dream Is Real

Behind the greeting lies a dream. The words we use in our greetings both cover and convey the hope we have. The dream haunts, echoes, bubbles and surfaces in all religions. All individuals and groups have their own dreams. But there is a special Bible dream.

The dream is about harmony instead of discord, oneness in place of division and peace ousting war. The dream is about what a human being can and ought to be, how a community could really be together, and how the world should be one.

There is a persistent vision of harmony, joy, well-being and prosperity which cannot be captured in any single word or idea in the Bible. A cluster of words is needed to carry the richness of this vision: love, truth, grace, blessing, justice, salvation, loyalty and righteousness. The term that in current discussion and in the Bible itself summarises that controlling vision is shalom. Shalom bears tremendous freight – the freight of a dream of God that resists all our tendencies to division, hostility, fear, and misery.

Shalom is the substance of the biblical vision of one community embracing all creation. The vision shalom carries is far greater than the English peace, the Latin *pax* or the Greek *eirene*. It is cradled in the nursery of religions we call the Middle East. It is rooted back in the ancient traditions as it grows from the Sumerian *silem* and the Akkadian *salamu*. It is echoed linguistically in the Arabic greeting *salaam*.

The dream is very real since the Hebrew shalom was originally applied to ordinary things and familiar matters. It meant *undivided* when it referred to inorganic objects like rocks and wood; *sound* and *healthy* when referring to living creatures; and *well-ordered* when applied to society.

In this way shalom links everyday life and faith. The completeness seen in nature, the wholeness sought in life and the harmony desired in relationships all moved naturally into the yearning for fulfilment, oneness and well-being for all which are the key-notes of shalom.

The vision of all people drawn into community around the will of God is the Old Testament theme. The New Testament has a parallel vision of all people being drawn under the lordship of Jesus and, therefore, into a single community. We are all to become children of a single family, members of a single tribe, heirs of a single hope, and bearers of a single destiny, namely, the care and management of all of God's creation.

The Dream Becomes a Prayer

Dreams lead to prayers and one example of this is Psalm 122. In the closing verses of this Psalm the word shalom appears three times and is linked twice with the city of Jerusalem (Jeru-shalom).

Pray for the **peace** of Jerusalem:
May those who love you prosper.
May there be **peace** inside your walls
and safety in your palaces.
For the sake of my relatives and friends
I say to Jerusalem, '**Peace** be with you!'
For the sake of the house of the Lord our God
I pray for your prosperity. (Ps 122:6–9)

Jerusalem, like shalom, is a heady blend of reality and dream. To this earthly city, pilgrims still journey. Centuries ago a section of the Psalms (Pss 120–134), known as the Songs of Ascent, were sung as the pilgrims approached or entered the city. In Psalm 122 the pilgrims arrive in great gladness, recount the story and significance of the city and pray for the shalom of Jerusalem.

This prayer is a dream that there may be harmony in the political and royal centres of power, unity between relatives and friends and an over-all completeness in the city where the presence of God is at the centre of all life. It is therefore a prayer-dream for both place and people. It is a ripple-prayer that begins with 'me', moves through the 'Lord's house' and into the social fabric of the entire city.

Limited it may be in its failure to reach out to the nation or the wider world. Hurtful it is when the acute divisions and tensions of the contemporary Jerusalem are experienced. But the dream persists, the pilgrims still journey and the prayer continues that the foundations of shalom will be present in individuals, the people of God and the whole city.

Our prayers reach out towards shalom. In intercession we lift the individual towards healing, the family into harmony, the nation towards unity and the world into oneness. In petition we see the gap between where we are and where we want to be and build a bridge of prayer that carries us further into the wholeness that is God's purpose for each life.

Many Levels

The human response to the Bible dream emerges at many
levels – in personal hope, family plans, neighbourhood
renewal, congregational vision, national aspiration and
world programmes.

Individuals dream – they want shalom. I have married
many couples, not all of them young! Practically every
wedding is filled with emotion as two become one, the
incompleteness of the single finds fulfilment in the unity of
male and female, and all the hopes and dreams are public. I
have walked into a delivery room immediately after the birth
of a child and been moved almost to tears by the shared
delight of creation and the realisation that the newly arrived
baby is the repository of so many hopes. Whether it be the
acquisition of education, the creation of a garden, the
making of music, the professional skill of the planner or the
eager dedication of the athlete – there is an in-built drive
towards achievement, fulfilment and completion. Individuals must dream – or perish. That is why anything that
damages or destroys dreams – whether it be unemployment
or poverty, racism or homelessness – is to be seen as against
the purpose of God.

Communities dream. Go to a tenants' meeting, listen to a
parents' get together in a school, belong to a League of
Hospital Friends, share in a political debate – you're into
shalom. Or you ought to be! When communities are
prevented, or diverted, from the realisation of a dream
sourness comes or anger erupts. Any inner city scene tells
you this story. Rioting is wrong, but it happens for a reason.
Strikes are debilitating, but they have causes. Cynicism is
erosive, but it often has a justification. When communities
stop dreaming they cease to have a future.

The world dreams. The United Nations Association is only
one expression of the desire that national hostilities and power
bloc suspicions will one day melt away. One of my friends is a
Norwegian doctor who has worked in Botswana, served in the
World Health Organisation and is now employed by the

Norwegian Ministry of Health – over the years our conversations have ranged over many subjects but all coalesce in the hope that, one day, everybody everywhere will have access to the medical skills and that there will be a lifting in the standards of health and the expectation of life. It is a dream that motivates and sustains many in the world of medicine.

In his book *The Songlines*[2] Bruce Chatwin writes about 'Songlines' or 'Dreaming-Tracks'. These are the names Europeans have given to the labyrinth of invisible pathways that meander all over Australia. To Aboriginals, they are the 'Footprints of the Ancestors' or the 'Way of the Law'. These trails are both intricate sources of personal identity and territorial markers.

These geographical markers have counterparts in other dimensions. 'Dreaming-Tracks' run through the inner life of each person, hold together the cultural oneness of communities, and move together into a world view. We all dream – and our dream is of, and for, shalom.

Appearing in Many Guises

The dream appears in many guises, wears a variety of faces and has a surprising persistence. The hope for wholeness and the vision of oneness can be illustrated in two contemporary examples – one to do with physical health and the other with spiritual truth.

In Britain the stress on holistic medicine has supplemented the comprehensive coverage of the National Health Service. It is the whole person who must be treated and the evidence is seen in the widespread reaction to 'symptom-only' concern and the mushrooming of the homeopathic and health centres in our streets. 'I want to be whole' – and 'I want to be seen as a whole person' are the cries of a sick human being who has an inner dream of health and well-being.

The British Holistic Medical Association, founded in 1983, says:

Holistic medicine means just that – 'whole medicine', taking the entire person into consideration – mind, body and spirit. It is an approach to health care which focuses on the uniqueness of the person rather than their disease.

Indeed, the holistic approach sees health as more than just the absence of disease, rather more a positive state of well being.

'Uniqueness of the person' and 'a positive state of well-being' are profound Christian convictions embodied in the shalom dream.

At the other end of the spectrum is the way-out 'New Age movement'. Glastonbury became the centre of this worldwide phenomenon in August 1987 as a 'harmonic convergence' of seers and seekers waiting for the new millenium was described:

Visionaries, seers, sages, pantomorphists, psychonosologists and plain old prophets are out in force with the healers, the fire dancers, the immortalists and the various travellers of the New Age movement. Everyone is a seeker of Truth, and there's room for everyone with a vision. Glastonbury this morning is the Clapham Common of the dream world. . . .[3]

Behind the fantasies and the weirdness the movement maintains that more people are trying to live their lives according to spiritual laws and there is a much greater cosmic awareness. Dreams persist.

The earthiness of holistic medicine and the esoteric nature of the New Age movement are both deeply rooted in personal hopes and dreams.

Add to all this the contemporary, and growing, concern for conservation and ecology expressed in the emergence of 'Green Parties'; the political quest for 'The Big Idea' that will replace Thatcherism which became a key note around the SDP, Liberal and Labour Conferences; and the evident vacuum of spirituality or philosophy in large sections of our society. Anyone who can shout 'I have a dream', as Martin Luther King did, will have an eager audience!

The hope for lasting and universal peace, which is the ultimate biblical dream at both personal and cosmic levels, springs from two different sources. There is the memory, often vividly preserved, of a vanished golden age at the beginning of time – and there is the natural longing of human beings for that tranquillity of order in which peace will prevail. These two sources stimulate and feed on each other. The hoped-for future is sketched in the colour of the vanished primordial age as it imagined to have been. This is graphically depicted in the Garden of Eden and the New Jerusalem metaphor, which, in our own country, is expressed in songs like *Jerusalem* – 'till we have built Jerusalem in England's green and pleasant land.'

Holds Together Past and Future

Dreams of this order are not to be dismissed as a delusion, daydream or fantasy. They are not hallucinations, illusions or the product of a fevered imagination. They are much more the aspirations, ambitions, design, goal and hope of our living. Deeply rooted in the past, strongly tugging towards the future – they grip us in the present.

These dreams, encapsulated in shalom, carry the qualities which mark the best of all visions – beauty, delight, joy and marvel. When Paul was writing to the church in Philippi he put together God's shalom, human dreams and life in a well-known passage that begins and ends with the shalom of God:

> God's **peace**, which is far beyond human understanding, will keep your hearts and minds safe in union with Christ Jesus. . . fill your minds with those things that are good and that deserve praise: things that are true, noble, right, pure, lovely and honourable. Put into practice what you learnt and received from me, both from my words and from my actions. And the God who gives us **peace** will be with you. (Phil 4:7–9)

The Scriptural basis for the dream or vision is much more

than the prayers of the Jewish pilgrims like Psalm 122 or Paul's hope for the Philippians. Shalom appears in the dreams that run through all human experience recorded in the Bible.

The shalom hope is used in the expectancy of a mother-to-be, in the looking ahead to the completion of a building like the Temple, and in the vision of a nation where 'righteousness and **peace** will embrace'. The dream spreads to cover peace on the borders, the hope that exiles will return home and the universal vision that the good news of peace will be preached to all.

Above all, the prophet is the agent of vision. In the Old Testament the prophet has no vested interest in the ways things are, has little effective power to change things, but does carry the vision of a new land and new people in the new age. The prophet points beyond himself to the God who is really in charge and will bring changes to human society. They look ahead to a future where God's reign will be seen by all people. Their hope is in the coming Messiah.

John the Baptist, the last of the prophets, links the Old Testament dream with the New Testament reality. He points to Jesus, who embodies the prophetic hope and is the Prince of Peace. He is welcomed in the Gospel of Luke as the one who will 'guide our steps into the path of **peace**', and will bring '**peace** on earth'. He is recognised by the old priest, Simeon; with the words:

> Now, Lord, you have kept your promise, and you may let your servant go in **peace**. (Lk 2:29)

This is the one who goes on to inaugurate the new covenant, who proclaims the Gospel of peace and becomes 'our **peace**'. He is the shalom person.

All this is made real for the first disciples and the early church. The Pentecost experience is described as the fulfilment of prophecy in Jesus and the giving of the Holy Spirit to all as the realisation of our dreams.

'Your young men will see visions, and your old men will have dreams' is the Old Testament prophecy of Joel 2:28

made real and quoted in the experience of Pentecost described in Acts 2:17. We follow in that succession.

This dream-in-reality is part of our proclamation – to all people at all levels. It will gather up, and include:

A personal experience
A corporate belonging
A world one-ness

It must answer the haunting hope within our contemporaries that there is 'someone there' and 'something worthwhile'. Writing in *Jerusalem the Golden* the novelist Margaret Drabble describes one woman . . .

. . . she would turn to quotations from the Bible, which appeared on the church notice boards, and on certain hoardings in the town centre, and which would declare, 'I am the way, the truth and the life', or 'straight is the gate and narrow is the way which leadeth unto life, and few there be that find it' or 'Man shall not live by bread alone'. These comforted her, not because she had any faith in their message, but because they were phrased with some beauty, they were made up of words that seemed to apply to some large and other world of other realities, and they bore witness, also, to the fact that somebody had thought it worth his while to put them up.

Just as some would pay for intelligence, so would others pay for the spirit. Even if the messages were not true (and she had no hope that they might be true) at least somebody believed sufficiently in their truth to pay cash for them, to rent hoardings and to put up posters for them, and that in itself offered some kind of alternative: Christianity meant nothing to her, but she was glad that in despite of her mother's defection, it existed.[4]

But that wistful vagueness has to be matched and answered by a distinct and visible life style that embodies the dream. At some point the inner dream must break through in the shalom character, the shalom community and the

shalom vision of the world in time. In all of these there is a
'living towards the vision'.

Living Towards a Vision

If we are to do God's word as well as talk about it, we need a
vision to guide us. That vision is shalom which, when
interpreted, experienced and applied to our daily lives, will
guide our attempts to work for justice, mercy and peace.

We need to dream new dreams and see new visions other-
wise we have no direction or purpose. That vision has to have
solid grounding in the biblical roots of our faith and face the
piercing exposure of contemporary *dis*ease.

I want to attest that this is happening. Dreams and visions
are still with us. I gather from the paper river that flows over
my desk evidence from just four sources:

● *Translating Vision into Reality* heads a report from a
theological college entering a new era of leadership.

● *Towards a New Vision of Church* is the title of a report for
the National Centre of Christian Communities and
Networks which gathers and disseminates news about
Christian groups, communities, associations and networks
which are trying to make faith meaningful in today's world.

● *Defining the Vision* is the banner headline of a
charismatic group moving teams into the inner city 'to co-
operate with the Spirit in the renewal of the Church'.

● *World Vision* is the umbrella title of an international
group of Christians engaged in relief and development
activities.

Four groups drawn from radically different theological
backgrounds, spanning UK inner city and the world, holding
together communities and colleges – all using the word
'Vision'.

But dreams and vision have to be earthed to be real.

A vision without a task is a dream
A task without a vision is drudgery
A vision and a task is the hope of the world.

Shalom is the announcement that God has a vision of how the world shall be and is not yet. Our double response to that is that we intend to discern God's vision of what the world shall be and that we mean to live towards that vision.

THE EARTHIANS

I had a dream last night
It was a beautiful dream
Unlike the American dream
Mine was a simple earthian one
I travelled from land to land
Without a passport,
I worked in fields and factories
Without a work permit
I was never called a nigger
A wop, wog, spick or greasy Greek
I was never put in jail
Kicked out or deported
For being an African or an Asian
An Arab or a Jew
A Greek or Turk
A Chinese or Vietnamese
Russian or American
There were no frontiers in my dreams
No barriers or Nationalism.
Instead only one land
One country, one nation
One continent, one planet
The planet earth
No chosen race
The earthians instead.
I woke up and heard the sad news
About Ireland and Vietnam
Cyprus and Ethiopia
Africa and the Middle East
Brixton and Tottenham . . .
Alas, my dream seemed impossible
so naive and childish.
Childish?

George Eugeniou

The Double Reality

Human kind cannot bear very much reality[1]
T. S. Eliot

The sense of discontinuity and disintegration, cultural and religious, current among many of us in the West apparently contrasts starkly with the basic Christian affirmation that all things finally hold together in one.[2]
Philip Sheldrake

Shalom is Positive

The word itself is misunderstood or prostituted. I talk to a banker in the City of London and mention 'shalom' – only to be told – 'Don't use that word here, we're an Arab bank!' I see a telex from Jerusalem and I notice the closing word is 'shalom' and I know that this word has come from a divided and disharmonious city.

Shalom may be a dream but it is very real. The roots of the word are in the market-place and the builder's yard. Commerce and construction are as real as you can get!

The word was used in the world of weights and measures; it is translated as 'honest' and in the sphere of trade has to do with the trustworthy, genuine and authentic.

The Lord hates people who use dishonest scales. He is happy with **honest** weights. (Prov 11:1)

In the shadowy, unreliable atmosphere of cheating and deceit the positive strength of shalom shines out.

Shalom appears in the detailed instructions given by Moses for the building of the altar in the promised land. At the heart of the worship there must be the soundness and security of stones that are untouched.

> Any altar you build for the Lord your God must be made of **uncut** stones. (Deut 27:6)

The threefold repetition of this instruction (Ex 20:25, Deut 27:6 and Josh 8:31) all stress that the stones used must be uncut (in shalom) because cut stones have lost their completeness and anything to do with the worship of the living God (whether priest, sacrifice or altar) must be perfect and whole. At these levels shalom is the word of wholeness, integrity and reality. Weights used must be genuine, stones used must be whole. There must be no distortion and no pretence.

Later, the word develops to include relationships and attitudes and the note of reality is never far away. They have to be 'for real'. This applies to the promises people make to each other or the covenant God offers His people. Harmony, wholeness, peace, completeness – all these are realities known to, or hungered for, by human beings.

Whenever shalom appears in the Bible it is positive and real. If used to describe physical objects like weights or stones it gives them a clear, definite shape and consistency. When applied to human beings shalom lights up the values, motives and attitudes that are life-enhancing and affirmative. Where it is linked with God there is an emphasis on the perfection, completeness and ultimate reality of His being.

The Negative Opposition

But that positive reality is countered by another. The forces arrayed against shalom are equally as real. When I began to write this book a friend wrote to tell me that I would need 'to coin an expression for the absence or opposite of shalom'.

He suggested un-shalom, non-shalom or anti-shalom but there is no one single word that gathers all the negative, destructive realities together.

The nearest I can get is in the use of English words beginning with the negative prefix 'dis':

disable	discontent	disintegrate
disagree	discord	disorder
disapprove	disease	displace
disarray	disgrace	disregard
disaster	disharmony	disrupt
disconnect	dishearten	disturb
	dishonour	

These are words that undo or reverse, deprive or spoil. They describe the process of shalom breakdown, whether that be personal or social.

We see social realities in the agenda that fills our newspapers and threatens our future whether it be in the national list of preoccupations:

The future of the NHS
Rise in violence
Problem of the homeless
Pluralist society
Affluence and poverty
Political and geographical divisions

or in the internationational headlines on one day:

Ethiopia's agony: will the world help?
UN talks fail to budge Iran's ceasefire
Armed gangs prop up Paraguay's dictator
Soviet radiation injuries continue
US team seeks answer to Liberia's economic mess
Israeli is accused of Arab girl's murder[3].

Shalom is absent from the national and international scene. Other realities intrude, displace and deprive. These can be personalised in human sin or understood as 'principalities and powers'. Even though we know and want to do what is right and loving, we often end up doing evil since we are part of evil situations and structures. These are expressed in the institutions of society and the patterns of social interaction, like racism, sexism and classism.

The Conflict in the Bible

The backcloth of order and disorder appears in Genesis, surfaces continually in individuals and relationships, disrupts nations and causes warfare, is seen starkly in the ministry and death of Jesus, continues in the life of the early church and comes to a climax in the book of Revelation where the central theme of the visions is clear – through Christ the Lord, God will finally and totally defeat all his enemies, including Satan, and will reward his faithful people with the blessings of a new heaven and a new earth when this victory is complete.

In Bible words 'we are not fighting against human beings but against the wicked spiritual forces in the heavenly world, the rulers, authorities, and cosmic powers of this dark age'.(Eph 6:12)

In the commentary of a modern Bible scholar:

In creation the forces of chaos are opposed by God's powerful will for orderly fruitfulness. In historic community the forces of injustice and exploitation are opposed by God's will for responsible, equitable justice, which yields security. In personal existence, driven, anxious, self-seeking is opposed by God's will for genuine caring. The biblical vision of shalom functions always as a firm rejection of values and life-styles that seek security and well-being in manipulative ways at the expense of another part of creation, another part of the community, or a brother or sister. The vision of the biblical way affirms that communal well-being comes by living God's dream and not by idolatrous self-aggrandizement.[4]

On one side there is the God-given drive towards harmony and unity that flows from the nature of God himself. He is shalom. That is why the Old Testament leader, Gideon, carves out his credo on the altar:

The Lord is **peace**. (Judg 6:24)

Out of his fear and uncertainties and in the face of overwhelming opposition Gideon holds to the undergirding reality of shalom.

This reality is expressed and carried in the dream of individuals, community and creation woven together in a tapestry of wholeness and well-being. This reality is taught in the Hebrew Torah, proclaimed by the prophets and embodied in Jesus who is 'our peace'.

Over against this is the multiheaded hydra of evil that flails away at this vision, fracturing and poisoning. The direct robustness of the Bible faces the reality of all these forces and factors that destroy shalom. This negative opposition takes many forms – disease, disloyalty, war, fear, over-activity, despair and sin are but a few (and are set out in the Bible Quarry, p. 150).

Two Bible examples illustrate the loss of shalom. One is social and other personal. When Ezekiel writes about national conditions he is astonishingly contemporary:

Everything is in confusion – the land is full of murders and the cities are full of violence . . . Despair is coming. You will look for **peace** and never find it. One disaster will follow another, and a steady stream of bad news will pour in. (Ezek 7:23–26)

As Isaiah proclaims God's plan for his people and his promise of help and healing he twice uses a sharp sentence to remind us that individuals can reject or lose shalom:

There is no **safety** for sinners. (Is 48:22; 57:21)

Both prophets understand, and graphically portray, the double-sided experience of reality. There is a New Testament cameo that depicts this two-sided reality. The well-known story of the entry of Jesus into the city of Jerusalem on Palm Sunday recorded in Luke 19:37–44 refers twice to shalom. The first time is in the singing of the disciples:

God bless the King who comes in the name of the Lord! **Peace** in heaven and glory to God. (Lk 19:38)

Here is the excitement of men who are walking with the shalom person. In him they both see and receive shalom. But they, and the cheering crowds (possibly chanting Psalm 122) are silenced by the words of Jesus, accompanied by his tears, as he looks down on the city:

If you only knew today what is needed for **peace**. (Lk 19:42)

Shalom was not at the centre of the city of Jerusalem. Corruption and division had created a blindness and resistance – and the shalom person wept.

This cameo draws together a skein of realities. There is the geographical and historical centre of Israel; the long-held prophetic hope of the Messiah; the human and institutional failure; the shalom bearer Jesus; and the grief and the judgement. That which ought to be is not. The purpose of God is thwarted but the love of God flows through, round and over the barriers as Jesus enters the city to become 'our peace'.

The Battle Today

Today the coach-loads of pilgrims are decanted at the top of the Mount of Olives and, escorted by the knowledgeable guides, wind slowly down the hill to the Garden of Gethsemane. Half-way down, there is a right hand turn into the Dominus Flevit Avenue and, at this point, stands the tear-shaped chapel. Below you sprawls the walled city, divided into quarters (Jewish, Muslim, Armenian and Christian) where national and religious tensions can be felt. Beside you stands the polyglot crowds of tourists silenced and still. The biblical conflict runs directly into the battle we know today.

World news for Christmas 1987, covered Bethlehem, Nazareth and Jerusalem. Drifting smoke from burning tyres and tear gas, the sounds of shouts and shots and the sight of street confrontation brought the reality of Israeli–Arab conflict into our sitting rooms. Underlying tensions and national hostilities surfaced in disturbance and oppression. But this is not confined to Israel – or to the pages of the Bible.

That double-sided reality is still with us. On one side we know only too well the breakdown and failure of shalom in every direction. On the other side we are aware of the yearning and reaching out for shalom seen in the personal search for wholeness and freedom, the community movement wrestling to uncover deeper realities of relationships and the world issues faced in the Third World or the Nuclear issue. These two sides can be seen in the microcosm of an individual's life or in the macrocosm of the inner city.

Six of our flats at Lawrence Hall were set aside for young couples who wanted to stay in East London and make a contribution to community life. They were 'diving board' flats designed to take two people on from marriage into ministry. Many of those who came have built a strong partnership and have become workers in this area. But one marriage ended in great hurt. We watched the young woman withdraw. She painted her entire flat dark-brown in one long night; she backed away from men, refusing to share a lift or exchange words; she was unable to share and communication broke down. Shalom had gone. But slowly three friends built bridges, created a ring of care, brought her into faith and eventually watched a baptism, a second marriage, the birth of a baby and, finally, a public act of dedication for the new family and child. In that one person we have seen the contemporary conflict take place and resolved.

But there are other battles. One is being fought in, and around, the inner cities. Here it is very easy to list the indicators that together have eaten away at shalom. Many have been presented so clearly and frequently that we are in danger of losing the message. The headlines are known:

Poverty and powerlessness.
Racism and violence.
Unemployment and injustice.
Homelessness and family breakdown.

Taken they make up a reality that bears down upon the lives of millions of people. For over 20 years I have lived as an observer-participant to this struggle in East London, able to list and categorise the forces that shape, and often spoil, human lives. If that were the only reality the prospects would be bleak. But over against these stand a whole panoply of concern and action that indicates that the quest for shalom, however hidden or misunderstood, is very much with us. Whether this is seen in Prince Charles commenting 'This is unacceptable' after his tour of Spitalfields in East London or in the belated response of the Government that puts inner city issues at the top of a national agenda, with the Prime Minister herself chairing the over-all committee. Whether it is seen in the urgent evangelism that initiates church planting and pleads for conversion or in the now widely accepted togetherness of evangelism and social action.

THE KINGDOM IS HERE

Lord Jesus, you brought us signs of the
Kingdom:
sight to the blind; healing to the sick
and good news to the poor.
Lord, we are glad.
THE KINGDOM IS HERE.

The poorest people, the sick and sad
were the ones who listened gladly to you
when you told them that God was near
and called them to come to his feast.
Lord, we are glad.
THE KINGDOM IS HERE.

We pray you to come to the blind and sick
and poor in body and mind today.
Give sight and healing and rich
satisfaction.
Give fruit of the soil and fruit of the soul.
Lord we are glad.
THE KINGDOM IS HERE.

We call you Lord and we want to be yours.
We know you have called us to be your
messengers.
Show us who we should go to,
the neediest people, wherever they are.
Lord, we are glad.
THE KINGDOM IS HERE.

In our own street and in far off places,
in crowded towns and in open country,
people long for sight and healing
and freedom from harsh oppression,
crippling poverty and a starved spirit.
Help us to find them and give them
your news.
Lord, we are glad.
THE KINGDOM IS HERE.

Let it be first with us to be true to you.
Then you will help us to forget
our preoccupation with our own security,
fortune and family concerns,
and to go with you to make real to others
the wealth of the Father's Kingdom.
Lord, we are glad.
THE KINGDOM IS HERE.[5]

Hugh Thomas

Gift of God

Shalom includes everything given by God in all areas of life[1].
New International Dictionary of New Testament

A great many people are trying to make peace, but that has already been done. God has not left it for us to do; all we have to do is to enter into it.[2]
Dwight L. Moodey

The Gift as Blessing

The experience of shalom may be conveyed in a greeting, held in the dream, and remain alive within contradictory realities – but it is always and ultimately the gift of God. We humans may work for it, dream about it and pray for it but, in the end it is a gift into which we enter.

It is a gift because it is a sharing of the completeness and harmony of God himself. It is the strong purpose of God that all should share in this wholeness; and those who live within that purpose know something of the oneness and well-being that is the very nature of God.

As we have seen, the classic shorthand summary of this position is Gideon's proclamation that 'The Lord is Shalom'. Others confirm Gideon's experience. Whether that be in the song of the Psalmist:

He promises **peace** to us, his own people . . . his saving presence will remain in our land. Love and faithfulness will meet; righteousness and **peace** will embrace. (Ps 85:8–10) or in the words of Job's friend:

> God is powerful; all must stand in awe of him; he keeps his
> heavenly kingdom in **peace**. (Job 25:1–2)

This experienced gift of shalom through the presence of the
living God flames out in the New Testament where the fear of
the disciples is countered with the constantly repeated words
of Jesus – '**Peace** be with you'. And, in each case, the peace is
in the presence.

The whole idea of shalom being gift of God, inextricably
linked with his presence, is most clearly seen in the famous
blessing in Numbers:

> May the Lord bless you and take care of you;
> May the Lord be kind and gracious to you;
> May the Lord look upon you with favour
> and give you **peace**. (Num 6:24–26)

This early blessing given for Moses to use in the life of the
people of God begins with the command of God – 'The Lord
commanded Moses to tell Aaron and his sons'; proclaims the
continuing care of the Lord; and ends with the final word
shalom, which sums up all other blessings. Here shalom is the
gift of God and is received in, and at, his presence.

These words, initially linked with Moses and passed on
through the priestly succession of Aaron and his sons, have
reached into our own day. They are often used in Christian
services of worship:

- To conclude a service, as a final blessing.

- To mark the birth of a child, whatever form of Christian
  initiation or welcome services we may use.

- In the practice of believer's baptism, immediately
  following the act of immersion.

- At the central point of the marriage vows, when human
  words and promises cease.

- With the laying on of hands in healing as a prayer for
  wholeness.

- In an act of commissioning or valediction, as the affirmation of a God-given task.

- As the final words of a funeral service, as those who mourn are pointed on to the eternal God who alone can overcome death.

Whenever, and however, it is used the blessing makes one thing very clear. Human beings require, especially at key points of their life, the favour and care of a living God. This gift is that of shalom. It is the giving of God himself to his creation. His wholeness is to be our experience. We cannot acquire this by our intellectual effort or moral striving – it is always a gift, beyond our understanding and undeserved.

But this blessing can be refused and the gift of shalom rejected. Shalom, therefore, is conditional. Whenever human beings live outside the purpose of God and flout his commands they lack his blessing. The gift is refused – or withdrawn.

Words that are the negative side of the blessing in Numbers are used during the exile:

I will no longer bless my people with **peace** or show them love and mercy. (Jer 16:5)

But where the gift is accepted and entered, where the presence of God is acknowledged and receives response shalom is known and shared. Consequences follow for the shalom person.

Bringing Prosperity and Reward

Shalom as the gift of God is much more than an inner experience, a warm glow! It stretches out to include physical and material well-being. Shalom itself is, in fact, often translated as 'prosperity' or 'reward'.

When the people of God sing of the coming victory of the Lord they look towards the day when God will give prosperity as men and women work with him:

You will give us **prosperity**, Lord, everything that we achieve is the result of what you do. (Is 26:12)

But this prosperity is far more than a gathering of material possessions. It has the time–eternity dimension and draws into itself a never-ending flow of richness:

I will bring you lasting **prosperity**; the wealth of the nations will flow to you like a river that never goes dry. (Is 66:12)

At one level, this personal prosperity and well-being is seen as the reward, or consequence, of personal loyalty and deep devotion. So that in the story of Ruth and Naomi, the family of the grateful Naomi (represented by Boaz) pray for Ruth; asking that her reward will be shalom:

May the Lord **reward** you for what you have done. May you have a full **reward** from the Lord God of Israel. (Ruth 2:12)

There is a double danger here, especially for those obsessed with the contemporary 'prosperity' stress. Outward prosperity cannot always be equated with inner shalom – whichever way that is read! The age-old question 'Why do the wicked prosper?' is still an uncomfortable dilemma. Some people's affluence does not seem to be a fair reward for their life style!

The other linked difficulty is the relationship between those who prosper and those who do not. The insistent biblical warnings about the futility of reliance on wealth go alongside the consistent affirmation that God is on the side of the poor. I find these awkward, unresolved questions. Believing that it is the purpose of the creator God to gift life, well-being, and wholeness to all his creation I accept that those who live in shalom should enter into a richness of experience that spans material possessions, bodily health and cultural resources. But it does not always happen! Where the expected consequences do not occur I have to ask how far the self-centred, acquisitive side of society (of which I am very much a part) actually denies shalom to those who should receive it.

There is something fundamentally unfair in the polarisation

we all see in the Third World and which I see at first hand in the inner city. The question of the 'haves' and the 'have nots' is not an academic question. It has to do with real people in real situations. And somehow this is linked with the relationship between a shalom that is both personal and social and whether the two can be so neatly divided.

Holding Together Personal and Corporate

The constant interchange between the experience of the individual and the well-being of the group is a profound biblical insight which surfaces in the way shalom is personally received but corporately shared.

In the Psalms both emphases run alongside each other. The individual's knowledge of shalom as a gift from God is expressed in Psalm 4.

> When I lie down, I go to sleep in **peace**;
> You alone, O Lord, keep me perfectly safe. (Ps 4:8)

It is a Psalm by a troubled man who is kept awake by his fears and his questions but finds his peace in the presence of God.

The other side of the equation, the gift of shalom to a people or group is seen in Psalm 29:

> The Lord gives strength to his people and blesses them with **peace** (Ps 29:11)

concludes a tumultuous Psalm that covers everything from the desert to the oceans and glimpses (like Psalm 46) the presence of shalom at the heart of a storm. The gift of strength and peace to the group find even more vivid expression in the story of Jesus stilling the storm for his disciples.

Nor is this only to be discovered in the world of the Psalms or the New Testament. One of the songs recorded in our local Rathbone Market and included in the *Songs of Praise* programme in September 1987 was Graham Kendrick's 'O

Lord, your tenderness'. In that song about receiving God's love the line of the solo singer:

'O Lord, I receive your love'

is immediately taken up in the crowd response

'O Lord, we receive your love'.

This song was the subject of the first phone call I received after the programme from an agnostic school teacher in South London. Behind his request for the music was a much more urgent search for the shalom love of which we had sung and for which he sought. For him it was a personal, intense quest.

But those of us there that day will always remember the market stalls, tower blocks and traffic within which East London Christians sang again of the gift of shalom. We knew that this has to be personally known, shared together, and offered to all.

I had been asked to take part in the programme and was interviewed on the roof of Lawrence Hall. From there we looked at the closed factories, tightly-packed houses and the changing face of London's docklands. Beneath my feet were the rooms where individuals lived, the halls where new congregations had come into being, and around us were the hundreds of thousands of people drawn together in just one part of London.

In the closing blessing I prayed:

Our Father God
We have sung your praise in the market place
Help us to work together with You in this community.
May all people know the wholeness
That is your purpose
For each person
And for the entire earth.

Always Embodied and Earthed

Whether it be *Songs of Praise* in the market place or the birth of Jesus in a stable the wholeness or shalom of God has to be embodied or earthed. It is not a vague, ethereal miasma – it has to be seen, touched and handled.

I owe a debt to the Iona Community. In 1956 I visited this island off the west Scottish coast where Columba planted the seeds of Celtic Christianity. The wild, natural beauty held the Abbey where workers from the inner cities of Scotland gathered for reflection and study before returning to the mainland.

George McLeod, the founder of Iona, delighted in the story about the stained glass window inscribed 'Glory to God in the highest' which had the 'e' broken to become 'Glory to God in the high st'. This, said George McLeod, was a necessary, theological act!

There is a constant biblical refrain about the earthing of God, making the Word flesh, becoming one with us. For a people aware of their geographical position and dependent upon agriculture God's purpose had to be as basic as the soil and tied in with seedtime and harvest. Shalom had to be known amid the fear of wild animals and apprehension about marauders:

> I will give you **peace** in your land, and you will sleep without being afraid of anyone. (Lev 26:6)

When the people of God found themselves in exile and in towns and cities prophets like Jeremiah urged them to work for the shalom of the cities where they found themselves and promised, in the name of God, that the characteristics of shalom would be known in the urban environment:

> I will heal this city and its people and restore them to health. I will show them abundant **peace** and security. (Jer 33:6)

And when the pilgrim return began and the people movement took place from Babylon to Israel one of the classic chapters about God's offer of mercy ends with the words:

> You will leave Babylon with joy; You will be led out of the city in **peace**. (Is 55:12)

Whether human beings find themselves in the country, the city or journeying the gift of shalom is to be theirs. But shalom needs to be embodied and fleshed in human form before it can be fully grasped or received. There are hints of a shalom person early in the Old Testament when God promises David:

> You will have a son who will rule in **peace**, because I will give him **peace** from all his enemies. His name will be **Solomon** because during his reign I will give Israel peace and security. (1 Chr 22:9)

The fact that the name Solomon is formed from shalom is deeply significant. In him the purpose of God is to be worked out.

His failure added urgency to the prophetic hope that one would eventually be born in Israel who would himself be:

> Prince of **Peace**
> His royal power will continue to grow;
> his kingdom will always be at **peace**. (Is 9:6–7)

It is John the Baptist, the bridge-man between the Old and New Testaments and the last of the prophets who speaks of the one who will

> guide our steps into the path of **peace**. (Lk 1:79)

While Luke accompanies the birth of Jesus with the angelic song

> **peace** on earth (Lk 2:14)

and ends the birth-narrative with the thanksgiving of the old priest Simeon:

> Now, Lord, you have kept your promise,
> and you may let your servant go in **peace**. (Lk 2:29)

Later still, Paul writes to the church in Ephesus about the way Jesus Christ embodied shalom:

> Christ himself has brought us **peace** by making Jews and Gentiles one people . . . in order to create out of the two races one new people in union with himself, in this way making **peace**. So Christ came and preached the Good News of **peace** to all . . . (Eph 2:14–17)

which itself picks up the words of Isaiah

I offer **peace** to all, both near and far. (Is 57:19)

Penetrating All

This continuing and powerful gift of God can change every part of our lives. In this surge towards harmony and completion that is the purpose of God for all people there is the gathering together of the wholeness of life. Nothing is to be excluded, all is to be drawn together in the oneness of spirit, soul, and body.

May the God who gives us **peace** make you holy in every way and keep your whole being – spirit, soul, and body – free from every fault at the coming of our Lord Jesus Christ. (1 Thes 5:23)

This gift permeates time, is made known in Jesus, and expressed in the covenant so that the writer to the Hebrews can say:

God has raised from death our Lord Jesus, who is the Great Shepherd of the sheep as the result of his sacrificial death, by which the eternal covenant is sealed. May the God of **peace** provide you with every good thing you need in order to do his will, and may He, through Jesus Christ, do in us what pleases Him, and to Christ be glory for ever and ever. Amen. (Heb 13:20–21)

All that we need to know about shalom we find in Jesus. In him, the word shalom becomes flesh. That is why we can look back and see shalom in action through him. That is why we can look around us and see signs of shalom in individuals and communities. Like you, I have my own personal pantheon of shalom people. One I have already mentioned – Jim Punton. In a paper entitled 'What hope for shalom?' he sees shalom as the key to the life of Jesus:

The mission of Jesus included heralding the reign of God; demonstrating it; bearing signs of it in healing; in exposing and opposing the non-shalom of poverty, injustice, exploitation, racism, and idolatry of every kind; in identification with oppressed and powerless; in loving, sacrificial service; in discipling men and women within his new community of love. All these were shalom signs of the reign of God.

Jesus is God's prophet of shalom, the world's priest of shalom, and himself the King of shalom![3]

When we believe this nothing lies outside the scope of shalom. The false distinctions between secular and sacred, material and spiritual, body and soul drop away for all is from and for God. He is the God of shalom and we receive the shalom of God. The shalom of Christ is made real through the physical actuality of the cross and the time-based resurrection event. Through him comes a transforming of human–divine relationships;

> We have **peace** with God through our Lord Jesus Christ (Rom 5:1)

and a revolutionary change in human relationships:

> For Christ himself has brought us **peace** by making Jews and Gentiles one people. (Eph 2:14)

So, like a well-advertised beer, shalom reaches those parts that other themes do not reach! Penetrating into the deepest recesses of belief and faith and penetrating the whole gamut of human relationships and attitudes:

> Jesus came so that things might be as they ought to be both among people and between people and God and even in nature. Making things as they ought to be transforms existing relationships; new relationships take their place, relationships which are the basis of shalom.[4]

I have a visual aid which I often use when I talk about shalom. It is an oval piece of wood from Israel. At the centre is carved the word shalom, above that is poised a dove and scratched on the frame are palm branches. This came as a gift from an East London woman who was born a Jewess, became

a Christian and fulfilled a life-long hope in her journey to the
Holy Land. Everything in the symbol speaks to me of shalom
as God's gift and our response. In her gift and in his gift I
have come to understand that:

In the giver Old Testament and New Testament runs
together.

The gift was unexpected, undeserved but greatly valued.

The dove is a sign of the Holy Spirit who is at work in us to
create shalom.

The word itself is at the centre.

The palm branches speak of our human response in praise,
singing and offering.

Those of us who are Christians are still trying to work out,
and to work at, all that Jesus meant when he said to his
disciples:

> **Peace** is what I leave with you; it is my own **peace** that I
> give you. (Jn 14:27)

This beautiful Hebrew word (from a verb 'to bring to completeness',
'to make whole') speaks of a totally integrated life with health of body,
heart and mind, attuned to nature, open to others, in joy with God; of
sharing, mutuality and love; of justice, freedom, interdependence,
reciprocity.[5]

Jim Punton

Rooted in Us

It takes one to make war but two to make peace.
An Iraqi spokesman in the Gulf War

*May grace and **peace** be yours in full measure through
your knowledge of God and of Jesus our Lord.*
2 Pet 1:2

Earthed in Response

Greetings require a response; dreams need earthing; nothing
is real to us until it is our own; and gifts must be received.
That which is of God must be matched by that which is truly
human. Visibly, this is seen in the body language of worship.
Hands receiving bread and wine, a congregation standing
together, arms raised in praise or a head bowed in prayer –
grace and prayer fused together.

But shalom is much more than worship. Shalom penetrates
into every crevice of life, spilling over the confining walls,
reaching out to the whole of life and all creation. Nothing and
no one is to be separated from the healing gift. Shalom is for
real.

Reality is in root-striking, in the word (again) becoming
flesh. Faith must be earthed – on this planet, at this place, in
that person, at this time.

This is the place
and this is the time;
here and now God waits
to break into our experience;

> To change our minds,
> to change our lives,
> to change our ways

> This is the place
> as are all places;
> this is the time
> as are all times.[1]

Shalom, then, is the nexus where the wholeness of God interconnects with the whole of a human being. Like the minute funnelling connection of an egg-timer shalom draws through itself all the unimaginable richness and resources of God and passes this flow of life into every part of the receiver.

Shalom is the bond that transmits and unites. Shalom enters into human experience through people. Some – like Absalom and Solomon – are given names that indicate the purpose of their living. They are called to respond to the God of shalom with a life of shalom. Their positive response brings the affirmation of blessing, their failure brings judgement.

This is the dialogue in the book of Job. The friends of Job argue that his misfortunes must be a consequence of his sin and that he is 'out of shalom'. They plead with Job to respond in repentance before healing can take place:

> Now, Job, make **peace** with God and stop treating him like an enemy; if you do, then he will bless you. (Job 22:21)

When repentance has cleared away the barriers then shalom can flow. The human response is wrapped up in the over-all acknowledgement of worship – 'let praise ascend and grace descend'. In the sacrificial system of the Old Testament this is expressed in the physical offering of an animal; which is described in shalom terms.

> When anyone offers one of his cattle as a **fellowship offering** it is to be a bull or a cow without any defects. (Lev 3:1)

The New Testament takes a giant stride on:

> Offer yourselves as a living sacrifice to God, dedicated to his

service and pleasing to him. This is the true worship that
you should offer. (Rom 12:1)

This response-offering and the shalom life (characterised by
the ethics of gratitude) are to be the human side of the covenant
which is both an expression and an initiation of shalom.

The Covenant

The greater the revelation of the nature of God the greater the
human response. Shalom marches with the progressive
revelation of the living God that flows through the Old
Testament and emerges in the full revelation of God in Jesus
Christ. As this understanding and response is rooted in
human beings the word shalom takes constant steps in meaning – promise, vow, surrender, faithfulness, and obedience.

Worship is seen as one answer to the unveiling of God
which runs through the history of Israel – and one side of
worship is the keeping of a shalom promise:

O God, it is right for us to praise you in Zion and keep our
promises to you. (Ps 65:1)

But promise is strengthened to become a vow, a lasting and
binding commitment and shalom is often translated as vow:

When you make a **vow** to the Lord your God do not put off
doing what you promised; the Lord will hold you to your
vow, and it is a sin not to keep it. (Deut 23:21)

The keeping of promise or vow requires a faithfulness within
an existing relationship – 'I will be your God and you will be
my people' – which is stated, and then broken, by Solomon.
As Solomon (the shalom man) blesses the people of God as
they celebrate the completion of the Temple building he uses
shalom to mean faithful:

May you, his people, always be **faithful** to the Lord our
God, obeying all his laws and commands, as you do today.
(1 Kgs 8:61)

The tragedy of Solomon's own life lay in his failure to match his own life to this prayer. Later in life his sexual excesses and alliances through foreign marriages brought upon him the judgement of God:

> They made him turn away from God, and by the time he was old they had led him into the worship of foreign gods. He was not **faithful** to the Lord his God, as his father David had been. (1 Kgs 11:3–4)

Faithfulness, or loyalty within the covenant, is the outcome of obedience. If God be the Lord and we really see his transcendent power and glory our deepest response is the obedience born out of love. The more fully God reveals himself the more fully we respond. That is why the Ten Commandments are a real and rooted response to the glory of God. They have to do with our relationship with God and our relationships with others. At this level shalom becomes obedience. So when judges are appointed to legislate in Jerusalem and apply the law of the Lord their instructions are set in a shalom framework:

> You must perform your duties in the fear of the Lord, **faithfully obeying** him in everything you do. (2 Chr 19:9)

The obedient man is in shalom, the disobedient is outside shalom. The connection between shalom and covenant is so strong that there are times when the words become inter-changeable. Whoever is in the covenant is in shalom; whoever is in shalom is in the covenant. Sometimes the relationship of shalom is sealed by both parties in a covenant. Sometimes the covenant inaugurates a relationship of shalom. So that Ezekiel uses shalom to express the final prophetic insight on the inter-relationship of God and the people of God: as God speaks through him:

> I will make a covenant with them that guarantees their **security**. (Ez 34:25; 37:26)

While Isaiah adds together God's love and the covenant to make shalom:

My love for you will never end;
I will keep for ever my **promise of peace**. (Is 54:10)

Because we forget or fail the covenant relationship provision
is made for commemoration or renewal in both Old and New
Testament and through to today. Each communion service is
a recapitulation of vow and promise, and each year the
Methodists call their members to a covenant service framed to
recall and remind.

The shalom covenant is the distinctive biblical arena for the
way God is rooted in us and we in him. We do not operate in
a deterministic world in which everything is given and
ordained by divine fiat; nor do we live in a world in which
everything is made by us and is at our disposal. The truth of
the matter is that we are drawn into the hassle of the covenant
which is untidy, difficult to define but creating a dynamic
interchange of grace and response. The covenant, like
shalom, is a 'therefore' model. Both are replies to the giver
worked out in the mould of history and time. Both are deeply
personal experiences set in the created and social context.

Deep-seated in People

The covenant has to do with people. It is made for, and by,
people. Here is the priority. Here is the 'given' in both
methods (living letters known and read by all) and material
(the flesh that carries the embodied word).

Moses and Isaiah, Ruth and Esther, Joanna and Dorcas,
Peter and Cornelius. All sorts and conditions of people step
out from the Bible pages. Individuals, pairs, clusters or
groups; men, women, families and tribes; Jews, Gentiles and
foreigners. Here are the bridges used by God for this message
of shalom.

People are to be the ambassadors, heralds, messengers,
priests, nation. In them, and through them, the word is made
flesh. Let me share with you how it works out in the sphere I
know best.

In the urban scene the people group themselves under three

categories. There are the indigenous. These are the 'locals' who are streetwise, know the area and carry knowledge. They are accepted and accepting. There they are – belonging, rooted and speaking the language.

Alongside them range two other groupings. The incomers arrive from the outside world. Each carries a different set of values, a contrasting background of experience and a distinct ethos of expectation. Some will settle alongside the indigenous, belonging to, adding flavour, working with. Others are using the situation – they are only passing through, having a limited role, and can be in danger of using others as stepping stones.

With them come the immigrants. Because of their colour they are often highly visible, carry diverse cultures, arouse resentment and even hostility and can quickly become the scapegoat of the urban field. Yet they are part of a worldwide shaking-up process which is breaking the demarcation lines, carrying the Gospel and calling out shalom.

Jeremiah 29:4–14 is part of a letter written by the prophet to the people of God in exile and therefore in social turmoil. Within the letter are three key-notes:

God is at work in this.
Settle down to build homes and belong.
Work for the good (shalom) of the city.

The biblical messages are singularly apt in a world of mobility, refugees and exile. They speak sharply to those who move in and to those who decide to stay. They have to do with the fundamentals of life – who you are, where you belong, how you live and why you go on.

The traditional response to the question of mission in the urban areas of the UK has been that of elitism. In the past we worked 'to send in the best'. So the proliferation of settlements, the idea of a special phase of ministry (five years then move on!) and the provision of large groups of imported leaders led to an exclusivism on one side and dependency on the other. The limited role of the outsider has to be set alongside the strengths of the three main sections found in our congregations.

The indigenous require affirming and valuing. Wider
society has devalued and deskilled them. The people of God
have a different and distinct valuation – 'God must love
ordinary people, He made so many of them!' This will mean
the calling out of the gifts which are often hidden and even
denied. Each local person carries personal and social skills
and insights which are essential to mission. But they must be
encouraged to stay. The long standing, and easily accepted
notion that to be a Christian is to get on and to get out must
be challenged. In my own scene we built 6 double flats for
young couples and over a period of 12 years 34 couples of
varying churchmanship have stayed and settled in the area.
They have become agents of shalom.

And there has to be training within the context. Since
indigenous people are distanced from the rarefied and
threatening atmosphere of college life 'think tanks' have to
take place where they are. We have experiences in East
London of drawing together 24 potential leaders in our
Baptist churches and using evening and weekend time in local
situations to absorb what is happening, to reflect together on
the implications and to support each other in working at the
consequences for mission.

Incomers require a different emphasis. They have much to
unlearn for they bring with them freight from their past. Back
in the 1970s two members of the Evangelical Coalition for
Urban Mission prepared 'Notes for Incomers' which spelt out
very clearly some 'do's and don'ts' for those moving into the
urban scene. The old Socratic dictums – 'Know yourself,
accept yourself, be yourself' – need to be applied at two
levels. Incomers must work out where they are from and what
values they carry and they must also work at understanding
the culture into which they enter and the people with whom
they work.

This operates at several levels. Urban trails provide an
introduction to those from the outside. A carefully planned
walk, with stop-off points to meet those working and living in
the area, will introduce individuals to history and reality –
especially if they walk it in the company of the locals. Many

have begun in that way and then moved in to live in industrial
zones. There schemes like the East London Induction Course
have offered the opportunity of stepping back to look hard at
the past formative processes, the contemporary pressures and
what this does to men and women. But always the most
important aspect is that of attitude – beware of the manager!,
watch the imposition of middle class mores!

The immigrant comes with another set of motivations and
hopes. Many move into the British urban areas because that
is where housing and jobs have been available and where
their own people have settled. They bring their own identity
and need to stop, look, and listen. Because they are often both
visibly and linguistically obvious they stand out. But they are
often the carriers of fresh and vital faith and they bring a
renewing and widening component to our Christian groupings. Through them God is fertilising the urban garden and
as they settle they will convey insights like directness,
simplicity and concern.

Since the Latin word for bridge (*pontifex*) corresponds to
that for priest the doctrine of the priesthood of all believers fits
the whole picture of mission.

In the sacramental traditions human priests bring the glory
of God to the waiting human audience – and then turn back
to God, in a representative capacity, to carry the aspirations
and yearnings of the people to the living God. In this way they
are bridges for traffic between eternity and time and God and
people.

When all three strands of indigenous, incomer, and immigrant are woven together in a multi-hued and developing
tapestry we have a bridge of shalom to which many can relate.
Tangible, touching and relevant, this bridge of people is
crucial to any hope of urban church growth.

Carried in Task

Shalom is a gift and a task. It is an incredible gift that leads to
a most demanding task Christians call mission. This has to be

worked out in co-operation. Co-operation with God and each other for we are 'workers together with God'.

In the Bible shalom is seen most clearly when people come together or are concerned about a series of God-given tasks. In the Old Testament it is 'Out of Egypt', 'Into the Promised Land' or 'Living in Exile'; in the New Testament it is 'Going to the World', 'Living in the In-between' or 'Breaking the Barriers'. These tasks take the energy, gifts and hopes of many people and draw them together.

The Greek prefix '*sun*' meaning 'together with' occurs frequently in the Bible before verbs of action like work, wrestle, pray, run, love, walk or strive. This distinctive New Testament emphasis underlines the significance of partnership in task and togetherness in project. But it is often far from the truth.

The traditional picture of the heroic, single figure stands over against the committed cell or team. The sacrifical act done *for* instead of *with* is, paradoxically, easier than the more messy way of consensus and consultation. Since, in the past, the urban church, has offered help to the dependent and opportunity to the able the two groups have fused together in our congregations.

When I first came to East London a local vicar told me that the community gives to the church the people they cannot cope with. On one side, these are the frail, damaged, hurt people; on the other they are the aspirers wanting to learn articulation and skills and to get out. The two groups meet in the church – and feed on each other! A caricature? But with some truth.

This is now countered by the modern stress on two factors. At the church level the all-member, participatory 'calling out the gifts' approach leads to a better equipped, more able army of faith. At the level of society phrases like 'let the world set the agenda' and 'meeting an unmet need' convey an effort to be real.

The tasks of the urban Christian are, therefore, as wide as the Matthew 28 mandate – 'Go into all the world' – and as specific as the Luke 4 manifesto – poor, blind, oppressed etc.

In the inner cities the response in tasks is obvious and visible. In the world of relationships between black-led and mainstream churches we have projects like Zebra, Badger and Magpie – their names speaking for themselves. In the spheres of urban mission we have Frontier Youth Trust reaching out to alienated urban young people, the Evangelical Urban Training Programme equipping working class Christians to evangelise in their own culture. The Evangelical Christians for Racial Justice wrestling to bring together Christians of all colours and to face the insidious effect of racism and the Shaftesbury Project drawing together professionals and thinkers concerned about urban issues. They, in turn, have gathered themselves together in the Evangelical Coalition for Urban Mission which is but one of a cluster of coalitions like Jubilee, Christians against Poverty, COSPEC (Christian Organisations for Social, Political and Economic Change) which have sprung up in the UK in a defined attempt to bridge gaps and unite in action.

The British Telecom advertising for Cel Net is a contemporary image in the world of communications and an essay in bridge building which could be a useful title for what is happening in Christian circles. Messages are transmitted through cells and networks. The networks are now often in the coalitions, the cells are best illustrated by the base community.

The booklet 'Christian Outreach to the Urban Poor' that came from the 1980 Consultation on World Evangelisation concluded that the base community was *the* tool in urban mission:

> We believe the basic strategy for the evangelisation of the urban poor is the creation or renewal of communities in which Christians live and share equally with others. These communities function as a holistic redemptive presence among the poor, operate under indigenous leadership, demonstrate God's love, and invite men, women and children to repentance, faith and participation in God's Kingdom.[2]

These communities are 'two-legged' in the way they hold together the Bible and neighbourhood reality, relevant in style and agenda, centred in worship and lay leadership and emerging in all urban areas.

The image I have in my mind is that of the grid system for electricity. A visit to one sub-station was enough for me to feel the pulsating power, to glimpse the way that power ran into and from a central unit and how it was networked across the whole countryside. There was giving and receiving, local and national, inter-connection and separation – and over all hung an atmosphere of vibrant power.

Ingrained in Place

People do not live, and tasks are not carried through, in a vacuum. They are earthed, rooted, put in a setting. Sinai and Calvary, Jerusalem and Bethlehem, and Temple and Synagogue – all are places where shalom events occur or shalom experiences are known.

Places today have their own resonance. Canterbury and Iona, Keswick and Taize, Greenbelt and Spring Harvest . . . it was there, people say, something happened. Pilgrims en route to Jerusalem or Rome, Bradwell or Selby . . . for them place is a bridge of spirituality.

More locally, the associations that cluster round the church of marriage or baptism, of conversion or dedication, of ministry or service are powerful and long standing.

There is a spatial symbolism, a shalom of place. Person, task and place cohere in Jesus as he accomplishes the redemption of the world on a hill called Calvary. Everywhere echoes reverberate. Moses leads the people of God through the desert; the disciples receive their commission in Galilee.

But this is no 'throw back' to a remote and irrelevant situation. It is highly contemporary. Shalom is not built by our words or by paper. Traffic takes place through people, tasks and places in our own day. These are the ingredients of the 'how'. Nor is this a return to a nostalgic, past rural world. This is the urban scenario. Here are the Gospel Bridges of our own day.

I see the people who are the 'means of grace' in my own setting. They have names – Ron, Elsie, Richard and James. They are described as a beat-policeman, a black single parent, a local young man, a couple returning. Tasks gather them together – missions, centres, coalitions, networks, cells and congregations. Here are the programmes that tackle issues like racism, church planting or political involvements. And all are centred down in specific places – some are international like Iona and Taize, others are very local like the Crypt or Shalom Centre.

There is no other way known to me to build shalom unless there is a weaving together of people, tasks and places. This corresponds to the known nexus of human experience. Significant events are always remembered by the people (who), the happening (what) and the place (where).

Under the title *Healing Encountered in the City* Martin Wallace, an Anglican friend and leader in Newham, writes about 'insights from an urban perspective'. The booklet is about shalom in the community and the individual and in the foreword Jim Thompson, Bishop of Stepney, says:

> The great word 'shalom' is used to evoke that wholesome, life-giving, healing peace of God which comes from the power and the presence of God among us. Shalom is profoundly God's wish for his earth, and this does not just apply to individuals who suffer and need healing, but also to the community and the environment which are damaged and hurt by social inequality and injustice.
>
> Martin does not let us off the hook by saying that the healing ministry to which the Church is called is just an individual matter, but rightly moves on to say that we have a care for the whole society, which in itself is in desperate need of the healing shalom of God.[3]

If that shalom is to be truly rooted in us then we have to

learn how to make it personal, understand it is most experienced in sharing and work for it to become universal – available and known to all.

To a psalmist it could mean the material security known to a group of people living in community, while for Jeremiah it included the warmth and fulness of joy that one finds in true friendship. In that case the word 'shalom' covered the right relations which can ideally obtain amongst men living together in harmony. The noun 'shalom' can even refer to physical health (Gen 43:27) or to general welfare. . . What is true then as an experience possible to man, and between men and man, must be true also of that obtaining between God and man.[4]

G. A. F. Knight

Make It Personal

Because everyone will do what is right, there will be **peace and security** *for ever.*
God's people will be free from worries, and their homes **peaceful and safe.**

Is 32:17–18

This radiant word expressed superbly Yahweh's all-embracing concern for human welfare. In it, everything that made for wholeness was intertwined: health, right relationships, justice, physical safety, good harvest, prosperity, the presence of Yahweh. [1]

Alan Kreider

Personal Well-being

Right at the heart of shalom is personal well-being. This wholeness, completeness, and harmony is the birth right of all human beings. The loss of shalom is a profound personal tragedy as individual lives are blighted, diseased and even destroyed.

Shalom is a totally integrated life with health of body, heart, and mind. A shalom person is open to others, attuned to nature and in fellowship with God. Time and again in the Bible shalom really signifies bodily health or well-being.

This belief that each person can, and ought to, have shalom is seen in the questions we ask about each other and in the human experiences we all know.

The constant concern for personal shalom is seen in the stream of questions behind our greetings – 'how are you?'

'how do you do?' 'all right?' and in the widening enquiries
that follow about other people – 'How is she?' 'Are they
doing all right?' 'Is he doing well?'

These are often an echo of the constant use of shalom in the
questions that punctuate the Bible narratives. Mordecai is so
concerned about his kinswoman Esther that he walks in the
royal courtyard every day

> to find out how **she was getting on** and what was going to
> happen to her. (Esth 2:11)

Greetings are exchanged between Moses and his father-in-
law Jethro:

> They asked about each other's **health**. (Ex 18:7)

Enquiries are made and answered in family matters. Jacob
asks the shepherds how his uncle is in a simple question and
answer centred around shalom.

> 'Is he well?', he asked.
> 'He is **well**' they answered. (Gen 29:6)

The prophet Elisha is anxious about his wealthy woman
friend from Shunem and tells his servant to:

> Find out if **everything is all right** with her, her husband,
> and her son. (2 Kgs 4:26)

Our contemporary questions and concerns, however
abbreviated or perfunctory, still echo the deeply held belief
that being well is important and that the personal experience
of shalom ought to be the expected and normal way of life.

What we ask of others we want for ourselves. We know that
shalom is known, or not known, in our own experience. Being
'out of sorts', 'falling into depression', 'having a breakdown'
are all phrases that indicate that all is not well. We want to be
well – to have 'well-being'. And that well-being is much more
than an inner experience. It has to do with relationships – in
marriage, family and friendship circles. It has to be experienced in many ways – being at home, belonging, blessed and
fulfilled. To know this well-being barriers have to be

overcome and removed, we have to be made whole and understand salvation in all its depth. And all of this will lead us into a personal life style that will carry shalom.

At All Levels

The experience of shalom is to be known within all the levels of human relationships. Indeed, there is a strong argument that shalom is always corporate in expression, even if it be individual in experience. The truly alone person will find shalom difficult if not impossible to achieve – or receive.

Shalom in the one-to-oneness of human love was finally and fully defined in the words of Jesus, often used in our marriage services: 'The two shall become one'. But it was portrayed much earlier in the collection of love poems in the Old Testament known as The Song of Songs or The Song of Solomon where shalom is used to describe the intimate unity of lovers:

My lover knows that with him I find contentment and **peace**. (Song 8:10)

That is why a statement on sexuality (by the Evangelical Coalition on Sexuality) begins with a positive affirmation:

We affirm that human sexuality is a joyful gift of the Creator God. Sexual intercourse is a celebration of intimacy as well as procreation, intended to be enjoyed between one man and one woman in life long commitment, in the context of publicly recognised marriage.

Where this breaks down we have a statistical avalanche of divorces which is only part of the mountain of unhappiness and hurt growing from the failure of God's purpose of sexual shalom. Figures do not reach our feelings but people do. I do not forget the child who, in the tortuous months of marriage breakdown and separation, was brought to our Children's Centre by her father and collected by her mother and visibly and hurtfully changed from a sunny, outgoing child to an aggressive, disturbed little girl. Some years ago I gathered together 8 men and women whose marriages had broken up and for 6 weeks listened to the sharing of hurt that was almost too much to bear.

If shalom is God's purpose for marriage then unity in diversity is his pattern for the family. There are deep emotive undertones within all families and these feelings are often carried in the biblical use of shalom.

There is the poignant anxiety of a father seeking news about his rebellious son's safety after a battle as he twice breaks in to the reports about the victory with the question:

Is the young man Absalom **safe**? (2 Sam 18:29, 32)

and then, weeping publicly when he learns that his son has been killed and that father–son shalom irretrievably shattered – and using words that still carry intense emotion –

O my son! My son Absalom! Absalom, my son! If only I had died in your place, my son! Absalom, my son! (2 Sam 18:33)

At a much more mundane level the stories about Joseph and his family often use shalom as the key word in relationships, whether they be parent–child or brother–brother. So that when Jacob is concerned about the well-being of his sons he sends Joseph out with the request:

Go and see if your brothers are **safe** (Gen 37:14)

and when, later in the story, the exiled Joseph meets his brother

He asked about their father's **health** . . . 'How is he? Is he still alive and **well**?' They answered 'Your humble servant, our father, is still alive and **well**!' (Gen 43:27–28)

In the Bible, family life is much more extensive than the modern nuclear family and we see Moses asking his father-in-law Jethro for permission to find out about the well-being of the wider family

Let me go back to my relations in Egypt to see if they are still **alive**. (Ex 4:18)

If the well-being of the individual is inextricably bound up with the harmony and life of the family then we are seeing evidence of both the continuation and the breakdown of this aspect of shalom.

These are both powerfully expressed in the East London scene. The 'extended family', even under the impact of population mobility and changing attitudes, still surfaces in family rituals like funerals and in the expectation of the responsibilities of 'next-of-kin'. Alongside this has come the strong commitment among the Asian immigrants to the honour and care of their elderly, often going alongside surprise and shock at the English provision of homes for the old.

At another level altogether, the uncovering of child abuse and the psychological damage caused by incest within the family is a wound at the very heart of family life.

There is always the danger that marriage and the family are considered to be the only worthwhile relationships and it is fascinating to discover the way shalom is used in the wider fields of friendship, whether that be within, or across, the gender divides. In fact, those who are friends are said to be 'in shalom'.

The longstanding friendship between Elisha and the wealthy woman from Shunem is one example. The close friendship of David and Jonathan is another. In one chapter telling the story of the help Jonathan gives to David shalom is used four times.

David tells Jonathan:

If he says, 'All right', I will be **safe** (1 Sam 20:7)

and Jonathan responds by telling David that, if things go wrong he will

get you **safely** away (1 Sam 20:13)

and that he will plan to make sure

you are **safe** and can come out (1 Sam 20:21)

and as the two young men finally part and David flees from the vengeful Saul, Jonathan uses the word in the farewell

God be with you. (1 Sam 20:42)

In this one story shalom is used in the realm of friendship to denote safety and the presence of God.

Human relationships reach outside the family and beyond friendship into the wider communities. This sense of shalom is to be seen in the solidarity of the peer group, the comradeship of fellow-workers, the belonging-ness of a neighbourhood, and even the closed ranks of the professional disciplines! It can transcend national unities and even break across the generations to come.

Even the double-tongued enquiry King David made about the welfare of the husband of his mistress implies the acceptance of a commander's concern for his army:

David asked Uriah if Joab and the troops were **well**. (2 Sam 11:7)

While the closing verse of the Book of Esther has the note of the obituary in its comment about Mordecai:

He worked for the good of his people and for the **security** of their descendants. (Esth 10:3)

In Many Ways

Just as shalom can be traced within the developing relationships of the individual so it is experienced in various aspects of life. Even as the relational side of shalom moves from one-to-one through family and friendship to national and even eternal relationships so the experience of shalom spans the world of inner feelings, the external realities of prosperity and reaches out to the ultimate fulfilment and completion which is the human goal.

In the Old Testament shalom is often translated as 'safe and sound' or 'secure'. People should be able to come and go in security:

Jacob arrived **safely** (Gen 33:18)

and when they cannot do so something is seriously wrong.

> In those days no one could come and go in **safety** because
> there was trouble and disorder in every land. (2 Chron 15:5)

Open frontiers, safe streets, and freedom of movement take
place within an atmosphere of security. When older people say
'I don't feel safe in the streets at night', when women flock to
self-defence classes and when we talk about 'living defensively'
we are into a breakdown of shalom at street, city and national
level. When fear decides whether or who can go out at night,
when muggings become commonplace and when children are
kept under tight scrutiny we have lost the Bible dream:

> Once again old men and women, so old that they use a stick
> when they walk, will be sitting in the city squares. And the
> streets will again be full of boys and girls and playing. (Zech
> 8:4–5)

This sense of security acquires deep overtones when we
discover that there are many more references to returning
home safely than to journeying in security. There is a clear
association of home with shalom. So Jacob can start a journey
promising that

> if I return **safely** to my father's home, then you will be my
> God. (Gen 28:21)

The understandable association of 'coming home' with shalom
in its translations of security and belonging stresses the sense of
being 'safe from'.

> (You) have tried to make your own home **safe** from harm
> and danger. (Hab 2:9)

And Jesus himself links shalom with home in his parables
about the power of evil when he says that 'a family divided
itself falls apart' but

> When a strong man, with all his weapons ready, guards his
> own house, all his belongings are **safe**. (Lk 11:21)

Even when disturbance and disruption breaks the shalom there is to be opportunity for restoration and a return to the former sense of belonging.

There is a close connection between restoration and reward so that even one of the tormentors of Job, having assumed that Job's misfortunes are the consequences of sin, can urge him to turn and plead with God.

Then God will come and help you and restore your household as your **reward**. (Job 8:6)

But the idea of shalom as reward is carried even further in the Wisdom literature:

Those who are good are **rewarded** here on earth. (Prov 11:31)

The concept of 'being blessed' leads easily to seeing shalom as prosperity so that Jeremiah's letter to the exiles in Babylon can refer to God's plan for his people:

I alone know the plans I have for you, plans to bring you **prosperity** and not disaster, plans to bring about the future you hope for. (Jer 29:11)

And the Psalmist can write:

The humble will possess the land and enjoy **prosperity and peace**. (Ps 37:11)

So a human being in shalom is seen as a successful person who overcomes personal vilification and attack.

Success to you and those who help you! God is on your side.(1 Chr 12:18)

There is a clustering together of the ideas of reward, blessing and success to make up a picture of a wholeness of living, an inner sense of integration and an outer experience of well-being. These are seen as the characteristic features of a human being in shalom.

The idea of shalom as prosperity and success moves inevitably into fulness and fulfilment. Ultimately a person in shalom is a complete being. This is the purpose of God, as Job argues

He will **fulfil** what he has planned for me. (Job 23:14)

Ultimately, we are to be as God is – perfect.

Overcoming the Barriers

Since this feeling of prosperity or the experience of 'positive living' is often so far from modern man shalom is absent and there are barriers that prevent fulness and well-being. Some are within and others external. There are three obvious barriers to shalom that we all know – bitterness, fear and burden – together with the greatest human barrier of all, sin.

One barrier is bitterness. This inner corrosion damages both the object and the subject with rancour and resentment. There is a poisoning quality about bitterness that calls for forgiveness and healing.

Heal me and let me live. My bitterness will turn into **peace**. You save my life from all danger; you forgive all my sins. (Is 38:16–17)

Unresolved bitterness towards another person or group is often at the root of dis-ease and unhappiness. Revealed in the denigration of character, the loss of a balanced perspective and the refusal to maintain or re-establish relationships, personal bitterness sours many lives. Bitterness melts when prayer for the well-being, or shalom, of the individual is made. Genuine 'lifting' prayer at this level releases the feelings of the one praying, restores right attitudes and creates a different atmosphere. Try it!

Fear is seen as a barrier to shalom. There is a lessening of dignity, an inability to act and an inner disquietude which diminishes the person and cuts at the quality of life. Over against this is a constant biblical refrain of reassurance, for to be afraid is to be out of shalom.

Therefore the servant says to the brother of Joseph

Don't worry, **don't be afraid**. (Gen 43:23)

And Daniel receives the messenger of God who reminds him

God loves you, so **don't let anything worry** you or frighten you. (Dan 10:18)

The verbal reassurance of the Old Testament takes on a new note when the 'word is made flesh' in the New Testament and Jesus overcomes the fear that has destroyed the shalom of individuals:

Peace is what I leave with you; it is my own **peace** that I give you. I do not give it as the world does. Do not be worried and upset; do not be afraid. (Jn 14:27)

It is worth noting again that this peace–shalom is not the absence of fear but rather the presence of love. Boldness towards previously feared opposition or serenity in the face of an uncertain future are two of the consequences that follow shalom. Right at the heart of human fear is the matter of trust. Fear is often failure of trust. For years I have taught others (and myself!) to use the final prayer of the cross – 'Father, into your hands I commit my spirit' – as a prayer of trust before facing the darkness of the anaesthetic or the possibility of death. Whatever the cause of fear shalom is damaged unless that fear is faced and overcome.

The third obvious barrier to shalom is frequently found in contemporary Christians. Ever since Jesus invited his first disciples to

Come to me, all of you who are tired from carrying heavy loads, and I will give you rest. (Mt 11:28)

Christians have felt guilty about feeling burdened. The loss of well-being, the failure to cope, and the weariness that replaces enthusiasm all eat away at personal wholeness and become a barrier to shalom.

The latest term in this field is 'burn-out'. The term caught the public imagination in 1980 after the book *Burn-out: The High Cost of High Achievement* was published. One definition of burn-out is

The gradual but eventually severe or critical exhaustion or depletion of one's physical, mental, and/or spiritual resources by taxing one or more of them without providing time for recovering or recharging.

Causes of burn-out can be rooted internally in a psychological make-up that make it difficult or even impossible to deal creatively and flexibly with stressful events or externally in factors like noise, violence or catastrophes. But the key cause results from interaction with our environment, especially other people. Anyone who has direct and intensive contact with people and assumes a helping role is a candidate for burn-out. That can mean that often the person seeking to share shalom becomes the magnet for those forces which are anti-shalom.

The sense of burden often follows the breaking of the God-given pattern of shalom. Those who do not take a 'day off' have ignored the principle of the Sabbath – 'Stop doing what you are doing'; those who hold everything within themselves have forgotten the injunction – 'Share one another's burdens'; and those who act as if they alone were responsible for responsibility for God's kingdom need reminding that 'we are workers together with God'.

My first ministry was on a housing estate in Birmingham. Whenever I went to the minister's fraternal I shared my many headaches and heartaches. In one meeting I became acutely aware of the somewhat amused surveillance of a retired minister. When the meeting was finished he came over to me and said quietly 'leave a bit for God to do, laddie!' I have often failed to remember but I have never forgotten his words.

The final, and the most significant enemy of shalom is human sin. The sentence

There is no **safety** for sinners (Is 48:22; 57:21)

is a sharp reminder that one of the greatest barriers to personal shalom is our sin. The verse has come down into common language as 'There is no peace for the wicked' which is a direct quotation from the Authorised Version! The unforgiven person is outside of shalom, the sinful individual requires forgiveness before healing can take place. In the Bible the phrase ends a passage in which shalom is offered by God to all.

> I have seen how they acted, but I will heal them. I will lead them and help them, and I will comfort those who mourn. I offer **peace** to all, both near and far! I will heal my people. But evil men are like the restless sea, whose waves never stop rolling in, bringing filth and muck. 'There is no **safety** for sinners', says the Lord. (Is 57:18–21)

God's offer of shalom is open to all, it is universal. The universality of sin is covered by the universality of forgiveness.

When barriers are removed and forgiveness heals we are being made whole. That is the next stage of shalom.

However we define sin – 'missing the mark, moral failure, disobedience, falling short of the glory of God, or wickedness' – we cannot escape from the knowledge that the poisonous consequences of our sin attack and deface our sense of shalom. Since all have sinned shalom is not possible until repentance is matched by forgiveness and restoration follows our return to the ways of God. Since we all continue to sin we all know the struggle which is centred around the maintenance of shalom and the barriers we erect to the advance of shalom in, and through, our own lives.

Salvation – Being Made Whole

In the Hebrew Bible, shalom is well-being in every sense. This includes:

Prosperity	things go **well** (Ps 73:3)
Bodily health	I will heal them . . . I offer **peace** to all (Is 57:18–19)
Sleep	I go to sleep in **peace** (Ps 4:8)
Death	die in **peace** (Gen 15:15)

Although shalom may occur in a list of good things it is much more. There is a gathering together, a completion, and a wholeness in shalom. Perry Yoder in his book *Shalom: The Bible Word for Salvation, Justice, and Peace* helps us to see that:

> Shalom refers to a state of well-being, an all rightness, an okayness. But shalom can be even more positive than this. At some places, shalom points to more than things just being okay or all right; they're super! At these places, shalom refers to prosperity, or abundance. Indeed, the two meanings of okay and super easily shade into one another.[2]

When this level is reached and a human being is becoming what God intended, the word shalom begins to link with salvation. Since the words for save in the Old Testament refer to salvation from real historical, political and material distress and since the Exodus is the classic illustration of salvation we can easily see how shalom and salvation fuse together. As the Bible is the history of God's saving acts, and as salvation is central to what God is about then shalom, as total well-being or wholeness, is the descriptive word for salvation.

That is why Jesus can link together the healing act, the response of faith and the consequent wholeness in his words to a woman:

> My daughter, your faith has made you well, go in **peace**, and be healed of your trouble. (Mk 5:34)

Shalom (and salvation!) are much greater than most of us believe.

Participation in shalom means sharing in the gifts of salvation, while expulsion from shalom means the end of wholeness. The Old Testament writers understood that:

> I have forgotten what health and **peace** and happiness are. I have not much longer to live; my hope in the Lord is gone. (Lam 3:17–18)

While Paul writes lyrically of what it means to be saved:

> Now that we have been put right with God through faith, we have **peace** with God through our Lord Jesus Christ (Rom 5:1)

and clearly sees that God's saving act which is answered by human faith leads into the experience of shalom.

The dream of shalom is, therefore, realised in salvation. Salvation for a human being in time is partial and relative. The full wholeness that is the end of salvation and the experience of shalom is both personal and social, individual and corporate. Salvation is much more than man's relationship with God. It is that – but it covers the totality (body, mind and spirit) of the individual, together with the relationships and economic setting of all lives.

That is why the words said by Jesus to the woman in the home of Simon the Pharisee have to do with a specific event and a continuing pilgrimage:

Your faith has saved you; go in **peace**. (Lk 7:50)

Forgiveness and faith come together. Through Jesus, the woman is made whole, knows salvation and begins a journey that is described in 2 Corinthians 5, which is a graphic pen-picture of shalom:

When anyone is joined to Christ, he is a new being; the old is gone, the new has come. All this is done by God, who through Christ changed us from enemies into his friends and gave us the task of making others his friends also. Our message is that God was making all mankind his friends through Christ. (2 Cor 5:17–19)

Christians know that final shalom (like full salvation) is beyond time and the gathering together of all nations and all the earth under the Lordship of Jesus Christ has still to come. But they already know the reality of salvation and shalom. This knowledge leads them into a way of life which is the shalom life style.

The Shalom Life Style

According to the Book of Proverbs it is the wise person who chooses to live in shalom and it is the unwise person who turns away from shalom.

If you refuse good advice, you are asking for trouble, follow it and you are **safe**. (Prov 13:13)

Wisdom can make your life pleasant and lead you **safely** through it. (Prov 3:17)

The wise person will accept two guidelines in working out the appropriate and responsive life style. The first is that of obedience – the shalom person's response to the authority and guidance of the living God which is set out by David for the people of God:

So now, my people, in the presence of our God and of this assembly of all Israel, the Lord's people, I charge you to **obey carefully** everything that the Lord our God has commanded us, so that you may continue to possess this good land and so that you may hand it on to succeeding generations for ever. (1 Chr 28:8)

And this obedience is seen in the dedication to the Torah, or Law of the Lord, which is the subject of the longest of all Psalms:

Those who love your law have perfect **security**, and there is nothing that can make them fall. I wait for you to save me, Lord, and I do what you command. (Ps 119:165–166)

Beginning with obedience and building on the teaching of the Scriptures the shalom person is drawn into a distinctive life style. Attitudes and actions, belief and behaviour, conviction and concern all blend together to create a shalom style of life.

This is a whole hearted, positive approach rather than a narrow, negative way. Too often Christians come across as carping, limiting, life-denying people. When I worked in the wholesale Potato Market at King's Cross, London, I found myself constantly serenaded by the porters with the negro spiritual:

There are three things I must not do
I must not gamble, smoke, or chew
I ain't a-going to grieve my Lord no more.

For them, Christianity was equated with a list of 'shalt nots' and was regarded as a negative, constraining code of behaviour.

Attitudes are the spring of action and our attitudes to people, to time, and to the world around us determine how we live and what we do. If you seriously believe that all human beings (including yourself) are of great worth to God; that there is an accountability to God for the use of time and possessions; and that you have been drawn into a renewed, re-created life by the Spirit of God – then your attitudes will be the motivation for your life.

There will be a simplicity in personal life style and sensitivity towards others. This simple life style will involve a stripping away of the unnecessary and an examination of the baggage we all carry. While this chapter was being written we moved home and we were astonished at the clutter of possessions, many of which we rarely, if ever, used. What is really disturbing about this experience is not the weight-carrying process but the inner knowledge that our affluence was the other side of someone else's poverty. Sensitivity within stewardship has been blunted by the too easily accepted standards of commercial advertising and the expectations of society.

The shalom life style carries with it a critical appraisal of what we have alongside a caring recognition of what others do not have. That is why the Evangelical Commitment to Simple Lifestyle moves from creation through stewardship to notes on a personal life style:

Our Christian obedience demands a simple lifestyle, irrespective of the needs of others. Nevertheless, the facts that 800 million people are destitute and that about 10,000 die of starvation every day make any other lifestyle indefensible. While some of us have been called to live among the poor, and others to open our homes to the needy, all of us are determined to develop a simpler lifestyle. We intend to re-examine our income and expenditure, in order to manage on less and give away more. We lay down no rules or regulations, for either ourselves or others. Yet we resolve to renounce waste and oppose extravagance in personal living, clothing and housing, travel and church buildings.[3]

But the shalom life style is only made real through the specific. In a world which frames judgements using the power of money and the status of housing as key codes the witness of another way of life is very potent.

Richard Foster, in *Money, Sex, and Power* writes about the dark and light sides of money:

The dark side of money inevitably leads to greed, which leads to vengeance, which leads to violence. The light side of money inevitably leads to generosity, which leads to magnanimity, which leads to shalom.

The great moral question of our time is how to move from greed to generosity, and from vengeance to magnanimity, and from violence to shalom. The vow of simplicity points the way. Simplicity gives us the perspective and the courage to stand against greed, vengeance, and violence. Simplicity gives us the framework to experience generosity, magnanimity, and shalom.[4]

A series of searching questions sharpens the point that the shalom life style covers all. How do we get our money? Where does it go? How much is given away? Do we practise stewardship? If we invest money, are we into ethical investment? What is in our Will?

The answer to these questions will give a profile that indicates how seriously we take shalom.

If money is one touchstone housing is another. The size and style is one thing, the situation is another. Where we live (and why) tells a story about attitudes and actions. Have we chosen to live among people or away from them? Did we move to 'better' ourselves or to be in a strategic place for mission? Is our home a place of closed doors or open hospitality?

Shalom has to be seen, to be made and to be made personal. I have been influenced by the Franciscans, known locally as the 'brown brothers' who have chosen to live simply where the pressures are – following the tradition of St Francis whose famous prayer is often used (and abused):

Lord, make me an instrument of your peace.
Where there is hatred, let me sow love
Where there is injury, pardon
Where there is doubt, faith
Where there is despair, hope
Where there is darkness, light
Where there is sadness, joy.

O Divine Master
Grant that I may not so much seek
To be consoled, as to console
To be understood, as to understand
To be loved, as to love
For it is in giving that we receive
It is in pardoning that we are pardoned
It is in dying that we are born to eternal life.

Illustrations of the reality of that response surface everywhere. Out of the riots of St Paul's, Bristol came this message:

We speak as Christians as well as people who live and work in St. Paul's. The Christian faith is about the way we live together in community. The God of the Bible is continually seeking to bring order out of disorder, the order of justice, freedom and peace. God again and again had to stir his people out of a false peace and call for repentance, justice and reconciliation, which alone lead to true peace.[5]

Out of the Remembrance Day bombing at Enniskillen in Northern Ireland came the very public act of forgiveness from Gordon Wilson, the man who had held the hand of his dying daughter as they lay beneath the rubble.

My wife Joan and I do not bear any grudges. We do not hold any ill-will against those responsible for this. We see it as God's plan, even though we might not understand it. I shall pray for those people tonight and every night. God forgive them, for they know not what they do.[6]

In her 1987 Christmas Broadcast the Queen said that Gordon Wilson had 'impressed the whole world by the depth of his forgiveness'. But she also said that some of the letters in her daily post reflected the darker side of human nature:

> It is only too easy for passionate loyalty to one's own country, race, or religion, or even to one's favourite football team, to be corroded into intolerance, bigotry and ultimately into violence.[7]

The battle is not always as public or as dramatic. More often it is the grinding, relentless trench-warfare that leads to attrition and sterility. We see the sudden flash of deep-seated prejudice or look at the swathe of casualties that follow economic disaster. We set courage over against despair and discover serenity where we expected bitterness. All this is going on around you – and within you. Shalom is here but has yet to fully be. The Kingdom is here – but has yet to come.

Go forth into the world in peace: be of good courage; hold fast to that which is good; render to no man evil for evil; strengthen the faint-hearted; support the weak; help the afflicted; honour all men; love and serve the Lord, rejoicing in the power of the Holy Spirit.

For Sharing

Have the salt of friendship among yourselves, and live in
peace *with one another.*

Jesus to his disciples, Mark 9:50

*The Hebrew word shalom . . . a full-bodied concept
that resonates with wholeness, unity, balance. Gathering
in (but much broader than) peace, it means a harmonious, caring community with God at its centre as the
prime sustainer and most glorious inhabitant.*[1]

Richard Foster

The Central Theme

Shalom is for, and in, sharing – that is our theme here, the
central section of this book. While shalom is experienced
personally its main message is social and corporate. It has to
do with the togetherness of relationships, majoring on the
word friend. There is emphasis on living at peace (in shalom)
with each other and enmity and warfare are seen as
destructive of shalom. This sense of oneness has to be worked
out in the wider sphere of society as well as in the more
intimate family networks. In all this, the peacemaker is a
valued and key person.

This understanding is not reached easily. It strikes hard at
the Western stress on individualism and is even more
uncomfortable for the Christian reared in the belief that
'peace' is (only?) a personal relationship between God and
myself. Shalom is sharing and indivisible and is fractured
when some try to corner it at the expense of others.

There is a huge gulf between the Old Testament stress on the corporate and communal and the laughable, but common, Wessex prayer:

God bless me and me wife
Me son John and his wife
Us four
No more.

Somewhere on the road we have lost the biblical stress on the oneness of life and the togetherness of shalom. And in case there are those who think that this is an unjustified pushing back into scripture of contemporary urban experience I want to point out that this is the shared conclusion of Biblical Scholarship. Whether that be the classical work of Kittel in the *Theological Dictionary of the New Testament*:

When we consider the rich possibilities of shalom in the Old Testament we are struck by the negative fact that there is no specific text in which it denotes the specifically spiritual attitude of inward peace. There are, indeed, more passages in which it is used of groups rather than individuals . . . In the majority of examples, in which a reference is to a group, the term clearly denotes something which may be seen . . . We are forced to say that in its most common use shalom is an emphatically social concept.[2]

or in the more evangelical evidence of the *New International Dictionary of New Testament Theology* where we are told:

the Hebrew shalom is the opposite not so much of war as of any disturbance in the communal well-being of the nation . . . Shalom has a social dimension . . . and has a public significance far beyond the purely personal.

Evidence of this is found in the close association of shalom with righteousness; with the concrete ideas of law and judgement and even with public officials.[3]

God's purpose of shalom has to be worked out within human relationships and friendships; lived out publicly in society; taken up by those who are called to be peacemakers; and set out in a contemporary shalom agenda. When this occurs signs of hope bubble up in real situations and penetrate into every corner of social life.

In Relationships

The richest and oldest tradition of concern for peaceful human relationships exists within Judaean Christian history. The roots of this concern are found in the stories and teachings of the Bible. Here the biblical notion of peace is a strong sense of individual well-being completed in a harmonious, just community which is summed up in the word shalom.

The generalised statement is made real in the human details. Again and again, shalom is used to describe relationships in both the Old and New Testaments.

When Moses is overwhelmed by settling disputes and resolving tangled relationships he is urged by his father-in-law Jethro to appoint others to share in this task and they become judges so that

> all these people can go home with their **disputes settled** (in shalom) (Ex 18:23)

and, at another level, political relationships are involved when we are told that:

> King Jabin of Hazor was at **peace** with Heber's family. (Judg 4:17)

While, in the New Testament, Paul tells the Roman Christians:

> We must always aim at those things that bring **peace** and that help to strengthen one another (Rom 14:19)

and the writer to the Hebrews urges his readers:

> Try **to be at peace** with everyone. (Heb 12:14)

It is the purpose of God that human beings should live in, and through, each other. Good relationships, at many levels, are the threads that are woven together to create the tapestry of shalom. Where that breaks down God moves to restore and those who receive afresh the gift of shalom are called to share that with others.

There is, therefore, a constant biblical pre-occupation which is expressed in the putting together of the key commands – 'Love God and love your neighbour'; in the picture of the new community recorded at the end of Acts 2; through the metaphor of the people of God being in one body (1 Cor 12); and in the prayer of Jesus, 'Father, I pray that they may be one' (Jn 17).

In our contemporary Christian world the sharing of shalom comes through in many ways and at different levels. It is especially seen in the practice of community, the charismatic movement and the culture churches.

● *Community* – a variety of models illustrate the necessity, possibility and richness of 'in-depth' relationships that range from the intentional communities (people living under an accepted code) to the network of committed households in a neighbourhood. The National Association of Christian Communities and Networks (NACCAN) has drawn together and listed many of these groups.

● *Charismatic* – this post-war stress on the work of the Holy Spirit, has a powerful emphasis on sharing, inter-personal relationships and wholeness. Breaking across the denominational boundaries, the movement has been positive in its release of gifts and stress on fellowship.

● *Culture* – in the cosmopolitan areas churches sharing a common language or a cultural background keep their identity and traditions by gathering together. In this way minority groups within our pluralist society retain and embody their own distinctive relationships.

But all Christian cells and congregations are to be visible signs of shalom sharing. The church is to carry and reflect the shalom gifts:

The **peace** that Christ gives is to guide you in the decisions you make; for it is to this **peace** that God has called you together in the one body. (Col 3:15)

To be 'in Christ' and the Christ-community is to participate freely with Christ in common life, embodying, developing, and demonstrating that shalom to which all creation has been summoned in Christ. This is the ultimate covenant relationship. This is

The **peace** that binds you together. (Eph 4:3)

In Friendship

The operative word for being in shalom is 'friends'. It is implied in the title of this book, which is itself the opening line of a song, which roots back to the scriptural model. To be friends is to be in shalom.

The use of the word shalom to mean friend, friendly, friendship is widespread. As strangers are confronted at the city gates they are allowed in with the comment

These men are **friendly** (Gen 34:21)

or they are challenged

The king wants to know if you come as a **friend**. (2 Kgs 9:18)

To be unfriendly is to be outside shalom. That is seen to be the attitude of the brothers to Joseph:

They hated their brother so much that they would not speak to him in a **friendly manner**. (Gen 37:4)

Betrayal is seen as the ultimate act of non-shalom, as when Jeremiah prophesies the defection of the court and supporters of King Zedekiah:

The king's best **friends** misled him, they overruled him. And now that his feet have sunk in the mud, his friends have left him. (Jer 38:22)

But it is Jesus who gathers together the strands in his saying:

> Have the salt of friendship among yourselves, and live in **peace** with one another. (Mk 9:50)

With this sentence Jesus concludes a conversation with his disciples that had begun with a divisive argument about 'who is the greatest'. It ends with the reminder that they are to live together in peace.

Paul picks up the theme (and the word) three times in his letters to Christians:

> Do everything possible on your part to live in **peace** with everybody. (Rom 12:18)

> Live in **peace**. And the God of love and peace will be with you. (2 Cor 13:11)

> Be at **peace** among yourselves. (1 Thes 5:13)

It is the purpose of God in Christ to change us from being enemies to being friends. The message is that God wills to make all mankind his friends through Christ.

In Society

Early on in the pilgrimage of the people of God there is a rippling out of shalom from the one-to-one relationship through the family into the kinship networks and out to surrounding social structures. The story of the wise woman shouting from a wall to the soldier Joab picks up the theme and the word shalom.

> Ours is a great city, one of the most **peaceful** and loyal in Israel. (2 Sam 20:19)

But it is the great prophets of Israel who lift shalom to even higher levels. When Isaiah addresses Jerusalem he links shalom with justice as the only way for rulers to avoid oppression:

> Your rulers will no longer oppress you; I will make them rule with justice and **peace**. (Is 60:17)

And even when exile comes to the people of God and they find themselves in an alien land as strangers they receive a letter from Jeremiah urging them to

> Work for the **good** of the cities where I have made you go as prisoners. Pray to me on their behalf, because if they are **prosperous**, you will be **prosperous** too. (Jer 29:7)

Twice in my lifetime this verse, where shalom is used three times, has come alive for me. Back in 1984, the European Baptist Federation meeting in Hamburg chose the theme 'Seek the Welfare of the City' and I shall always remember leading a workshop on urban mission in which my fellow Baptists (best known for their emphasis on personal conversion and the church as the gathered community) wrestled to apply this message to the cities of Europe. But, even more sharply, a Bible Study group on this passage from Jeremiah wrote letters to the Tamil group that had sung with us as a choir in *Songs of Praise from Newham*. We sent four letters to the Emmanuel Tamil Fellowship, urging them to settle into our community, to come together in the faith and to work for the shalom of the society in which they found themselves. Our group came alive as we saw afresh how relevant the theme of shalom was, especially in a divided, uncertain society. We had learnt for ourselves that shalom has to be worked out where we are, even if that be among strangers.

Wherever we are, absence of shalom and lack of harmony are expressed in social disorder as evidenced in economic inequality, injustice, political oppression or exclusivism. Look around to see it – where you live or in the wider affairs of the nation.

Becoming Peacemakers

When within the complex web of relationships intolerance erodes acceptance and hostility destroys unity the shalom people are called to be the peacemakers and reconcilers.

When warfare replaces welfare or poverty eats away at prosperity then the God-given ministry of making peace and sharing shalom begins.

There are many biblical precedents. The first Christian martyr, Stephen, uses the Old Testament example of Moses in his speech before the Council when he reminds his Jewish listeners that Moses intervened in a fight and that

He tried to make **peace** between them. (Acts 7:26)

But Stephen's death and his echoing of the words of Jesus on the cross: 'Do not remember this sin against them' becomes a New Testament example of peacemaking. Stephen's words and actions are in direct succession from Jesus who both taught and demonstrated the way of the peacemaker.

The collection of the sayings of Jesus known as the Sermon on the Mount opens with the Beatitudes and includes the famous sentence:

Happy are those who work for **peace**;
God will call them his children! (Mt 5:9)

This is better known in the Authorised Version: 'Blessed are the peacemakers' which has too often been narrowed down to peacekeeping. But Jesus is not talking about the passive quality of peaccableness or even the attitudes embodied in peace loving but the far stronger, outgoing task of making (manufacturing) shalom.

Peace making, in the biblical sense, is the highest of all tasks, linking up with the activity of God himself:

God is powerful; all must stand in awe of him;
he keeps his heavenly kingdom in **peace**. (Job 25:1–2)

Yet this heavenly activity is brought to earth with the coming of Jesus:

Glory to God in the highest heaven,
and **peace** on earth . . . (Lk 2:14)

It is shalom that connects the heavenly and earthly kingdoms. Jesus comes as the Prince of Peace and becomes the

peacemaker. He calls us into this shalom and invites us to be
workers together with him in the task of peacemaking. This
process is positive, fruitful and costly.

Peacemaking is positive. It is much more than the removal
of war or the absence of conflict. It is the presence of love and
the experience of shalom.

> We must stress that shalom is a positive idea. It points to
> the presence of something like well-being and health, rather
> than having mainly a negative focus like English peace
> which points to the absence of something like war. This is
> important, because in English we tend to define peace as
> the absence of something: turmoil, distress, or war; rather
> than the positive presence of things as they should be. This
> can result in a notion that peace-makers are passive,
> avoiding conflict and struggle. On the contrary, shalom
> making is being for something – for a new situation in
> which people are all right with their material needs being
> met. In this light, peacemaking as shalom making is
> striving so that those who do not now enjoy material
> shalom and physical well-being can do so.[4]

Peacemaking is fruitful. The close connection between faith
and fruit was made by Jesus: 'A healthy tree bears good fruit,
but a poor tree bears bad fruit' (Mt 7:17) and emphasised by
James: 'faith without actions is dead' (Jas 2:26). And it is
James who, in a vivid word-picture, spells out the harvest that
is the consequence of peacemaking:

> Goodness is the harvest that is produced from the seeds the
> **peacemakers** plant in **peace**. (Jas 3:18)

Peacemaking gives and does not take away; opens up rather
than shutting out; creates something fresh in place of the sour
sterility; and reaches out to break down all barriers and draw
all together.

But peacemaking is costly. In the New Testament peace is
inextricably tied to the Cross:

> God made **peace** through his Son's death on the cross and

so brought back to himself all things, both on earth and in heaven. (Col 1:20)

There is no cheap way. There is a price to be paid by the peacemakers. Whether that be in the effort to reconcile two embittered people, to bring together hostile groups or to bridge the frontiers of national separation. At the ultimate, universal level that cost is the unimaginable, overwhelming agony of the cross. In our tiny, but significant, contributions to peace-making there will be misunderstanding, rejection and hostility. It is easier to turn a blind eye or to move away. But that would be a denial of shalom.

In his book *Issues Facing Christians Today*, John Stott maintains that Christian peacemakers must set an example as a community of peace.

> God's call to us is not only to 'preach peace' and to 'make peace' but also to embody it. For his purpose, through the work of his Son and his Spirit, is to create a new reconciled society in which no curtains, walls or barriers are tolerated, and in which the divisive influences of race, nationality, rank and sex have been destroyed. He means his church to be a sign of his Kingdom, that is, a model of what human com-munity looks like when it comes under his rule of righteous-ness and peace. An authentic Kingdom community will then challenge the value system of the secular community and offer a viable alternative. We can hardly call the world to peace while the church falls short of being the reconciled community God intends it to be. If charity begins at home, so does reconciliation. We need to banish all malice, anger and bitterness from both church and home, and make them instead communities of love, joy and peace. The influence for peace of communities of peace is inestimable.[5]

The Shalom Agenda

The peacemaking agenda covers many issues and includes many people. Anyone seeking to live in, and by, shalom, will be drawn into a fresh understanding of the attitudes behind, and the action required, in the ministry of reconciliation.

Take planning. In a small island like Britain whatever happens in one area has a 'knock-on' effect in another. The effect of the Chunnel will not be confined to the Kentish coast and the M25 is not merely another road! Inner city concerns are not only for those who live there plus a few interested people. They affect us all. Development in the countryside is not merely an issue between those who already live there fighting to safeguard the rural peace and those who want to move out to a better environment to secure the well-being of their families. What is built and who moves in impinges on all of us.

We journey regularly between East London and Eversley in North East Hampshire. A controversy about 'some planning in the South East' has grown up around the proposal to build yet more townships between the M4 and Basingstoke. A letter from the treasurer of the lobby against this move wrote to local people:

> We have all seen and felt the consequences of unplanned development in parts of this region and we have all heard the pleas for the regeneration of the centres of our great cities. If the former are allowed to proceed unchecked it will be at the expense of the latter and of us all, wherever we live.

The biblical principles that the 'earth is the Lord's' and that we are stewards before God takes into account the well-being, or shalom, of all. There is to be a sharing of concern before there is allocation of resources.

Look more closely at economics and politics. Rate-capping is about national and local shalom. If financial resources are not distributed in response to need rather than possession we break shalom. A positive feature of the contemporary church is the way many Christians are, at last, seriously addressing the awkward issues of power and finance. So the director of the evangelical Shaftesbury Project can launch a new initiative for local churches by saying:

> We see our role in the future, as enabling the local church
> to take action on social, economic and political issues so
> that it can become the major force in modern society that
> we all believe it should be.

And at a much more local level I became involved in the rate-
capping issue when the Minister for the Environment,
Rhodes Boyson, was brought to Lawrence Hall. Politicians,
council officers, and MPs were asked to withdraw while three
of us from the voluntary sector (the director of the Voluntary
Agencies Council, the Anglican Borough Dean and myself)
showed the Minister examples of partnership, shared our
concern at the consequences of the proposed rate-capping and
argued from the basis of shalom that the welfare of the
weakest in our community must be a concern for those
involved in both national and local politics.

Think again about racism. The Joint Christian Group on
Race Relations prepared for the General Election of 1987 by
reminding us that

> Christians are committed to the belief that all human
> beings are of equal value to God, and what they do towards
> other human beings is done towards God Himself. We are
> supposed to look after each other, to do justice, show
> mercy, be open and generous, ready both to give and to
> accept.[6]

Our society is a long way from this hope. Young black men
are twice as likely to be unemployed as young white men.
Racial violence against people from the Indian sub-continent,
the Caribbean and Vietnam is on a horrifying scale. In 1981
the Home Office estimated that black people were 50 or 60
times more likely than white people to be the victims of
racially motivated 'incidents' – but in 1984 the Policy Studies
Institute concluded from its own research that the Home
Office had underestimated racial attacks on black people by
as much as ten times.

Thousands of families are kept permanently divided,
parents from children and husbands from wives, by the
operation of the immigration law, and these families are

virtually all non-white. Bring this down to street level and talk to individuals and the detachment of reports and words breaks down in face of the experiences and emotions.

Planning, economics and race-relations are only three items on the shalom agenda. Attitudes and actions that are rooted in shalom will apply to all social issues. Some, like politics, economics, international relationships and world poverty, are huge and multi-dimensional.

Others, like sexuality or disability are more personal and day-to-day. Check out sexuality. Gender issues are tied up with shalom. The harmony between two individuals in marriage, the unity of the family, and status at work are all linked to the convictions and attitudes that flow from the shalom principle. Issues like equality, interdependence and authority are all tied into the male–female debate. Why do we need workshops on 'Assertiveness for Women' and 'Sensitivity for Men'? Shalom has yet to become fully worked out between the sexes.

Think again about the disabled. A recent report *Poverty and Disability* came to the crushing conclusion that two-thirds of disabled people live at or below the poverty line. And this in a Welfare State!

Add your own items to the agenda. They will vary according to where you live, what you do and how widely you cast the shalom net.

Agendas for action will follow wherever the gift and task of shalom are taken seriously. A concern for individuals and structures will reach into every level and dimension of congregational and community life, swinging from local to national and out to global. These agendas will not be shaped by aggression or framed by the pursuit of power. Rather, 'the towel and the basin are symbols of shalom' and service and care will be the characteristics.

Signs of Hope

There are groups, congregations, networks and movements within our society which are committed to making peace. They are to be found at many levels of Christian action seeking to make shalom real for themselves and for others. As David Sheppard says:

> What is new in recent years is that Christian voices in these areas have challenged the whole church about its priorities and about its ways of believing and doing theology.

Here are some of these emphases, voices or signs of hope:

● The stress on the church as the Body of Christ – accepting and belonging, receiving and giving. The emergence of house groups, cells and the writing on 'the base community' all point to a rediscovery of togetherness, care and solidarity which are the marks of shalom.

● The emergence of the new churches, whether they be charismatic or cultural – underlining the corporate, teaching wholeness, gathering together in a richness of worship and fellowship.

● The community movement – in which the individual shares life as fully as possible with a small group within 'intentional community'. This can be seen in the neighbourhood home or in the national networks that reach out to hundreds of groups.

● The flood of literature on shalom where titles speak for themselves: *Justice on the Agenda*, *Bias to the Poor*, *Belief in a Mixed Society*, *Sharing Possessions*, *Down to Earth* . . .

● The rediscovery of the relevance and authority of Scripture – whether that be set out in the Lausanne Covenant, worked out in the Bible studies or thought through in publications like *Towards a Lost Bequest*, *Living Towards a Vision* or *Shalom: the Bible's Word for Salvation, Justice, Peace*.

● The accelerating response of the Churches towards issues like the inner city – expressed in the Anglican *Faith in the City Report* and its consequences and in the Methodist 'Two Nations, One Gospel' movement which led to *Mission Alongside the Poor* as well as the more localised Brixton Deanery Clergy whose statement after the riots said

We believe that because our people are facing daily many of the most urgent problems of this society – so their insights, their lessons, their testimony, have a profound importance for the wider Church . . . and beyond.

● The acknowledgement that we now live in a shrinking and cosmopolitan world – Ray Bakke, a leading exponent of Urban Mission, maintains in his book *The Urban Christian* that 'The Lord is shaking up the world'. In a review of world population and urbanisation he makes us see that the nations of the world are now in our cities.

● The thrusting-out of imaginative and dynamic agents of shalom – Amnesty International, CND, World Development Movement, Greenpeace, Christian Aid, Friends of the Earth.

● The wider acceptance in many quarters of those who stand with us in issues like 'Equal Opportunity', the Peace Movement or Ecology.

A PRAYER

In the aftermath of the riots in Handsworth a young man in his twenties sat in a meeting writing out a prayer. I have kept and reproduced that prayer because it is a manifesto for shalom in the face of a divided and violent society.

Lord, God of the Universe
Giver of life, Bearer of pain, Maker of love
We sit alongside those weak with weeping this morning
Broken in spirit and despairing of love
For you promised to be with the poor of Handsworth

We acknowledge our part in the chaos and violence
By our employment, they are thrown out of work
By our riches and power, they are made poor and powerless
By our privilege they are disadvantaged
By our racism, their very humanity is denied.

Yet in the presence of all that degrades and shatters people
Your life is there to bring consolation, support, gentle warmth.

Be with the injured police and fire officers – give them your healing.
Be with those arrested or detained – give them your justice.
Be with the fearful elderly or confused children – give them your word.
Be with the rioters who are at home – give them your forgiveness.
Be with those who have lost all by fire and looting – give them your presence.
Be with your people in Handsworth, that they may be the instruments of your peace.

Sovereign and Eternal Spirit, we ask for your justice and peace
relieve the unemployment, racism and deprivation of the poor in our land
touch the hearts of the rich, propertied and powerful with your free grace,
raise up peacemakers to draw communities into material harmony and honest exchange,
bring injustice, violence and intolerance to an end and make this world your own.

May your Commonwealth of Peace and Freedom sustain our hope and come on earth,
For you reign in the glory of the power that is love, now and for ever,
Amen.

To Be Universal

I am calling for a return to some model, some picture which takes the whole range of man's existence into account. And I still believe that the kingdom of right relationships, the society of the shalom of God, which was offered to mankind in the covenant he made with the Hebrew people, and later lived out in personal dimensions and made available to the whole world in Christ, is valid for the deep perplexities of our own day.[1]

John V. Taylor

I offer peace to all, both near and far.

Isaiah 57:19

Shalom is to cover the whole earth. It is to be the experience of each individual, the mark of personal relationships, the key feature of community life – and it is to be known within each nation, between nations and, ultimately, reach to the far corners of the earth.

The widening of the dream emerges slowly in the Old Testament. The early books are caught up in the individual and family life stories, to be followed by the tribal and 'chosen people' parameters. But the universality of shalom is hinted at in the Psalms, proclaimed by the prophets and set out in full in the New Testament. There the teaching of Jesus in the Gospels is geographically spread in the Book of Acts and thought through to a universal fulness in the Epistles.

The all-embracing nature of shalom moves inexorably from the individual through the group to the district. The worldwide rule of shalom begins with the life of the nation, must be known between nations, will finally cover the entire earth and ultimately embrace 'all things, both on earth and in heaven'.

It is obvious that the churches which have historically thought of sin, guilt and forgiveness in a narrow sense have settled for a very individualistic articulation of the gospel. Sin and forgiveness for the individual is fundamental but is too narrow a basis to face international peace or national economics. There is structural and national sin and, in the words of Raymond Fung, all are sinners but some are more sinned against.

If the purpose of God is to be carried through wholeness and well-being must cover the entire earth and penetrate every level of relationship. Personal, family, neighbourhood, nation, world and universe – that is the scope of shalom. The vision must be held, the newness must come.

> The world does not believe in newness. It believes that things must remain as they are. And for those of us well off, it is a deep hope that things will remain as they are. Every new emergent is quickly domesticated; and if it cannot be domesticated, it is outlawed or crushed.
>
> That is the bite in our faith and the crunch in our ministry. We are bearers of newness. But we address and, in part, ourselves constitute a world which has a low tolerance level for newness. But the faith community . . . exists precisely to announce the new, to affirm that we do not live by what is, but by what is promised. So the hassle goes on.[2]

We are committed to a whole earth of shalom. That must be within each nation, across the borders and, ultimately, over the entire planet.

Within the Nation

Psalm 72 is a prayer for the King of Israel that opens with a plea that he will judge with righteousness and rule with justice.

If that occurs then shalom will follow. That shalom will cover the whole land and will continue into the future.

At the national level, therefore, shalom is rooted and grounded in righteousness and justice and, in the Psalm, this has particular reference to the oppressed and to the poor.

Echoes of this come right down to our own day in the way we speak about 'the Queen's Peace' and in the use of the phrase 'Justice of the Peace' to describe a magistrate appointed to administer justice within the community, and in the way someone is 'bound over to keep the peace'.

But this is much more than the imposition of 'law and order'. It has to do with acceptance of each other, sharing of resources, harmony between groups, and the removal of injustice and inequality.

The idea of our nation being the United Kingdom sits uneasily on a divided society. Divisions betwen us are to be seen geographically, economically, socially and culturally. This is evident in rural deprivation as much as in inner city powerlessness. It is expressed in the difficulties of employment, the incidence of poverty and the limitations of choice that mark one area or group. It is illustrated in the political divide revealed by the General Election. We are not one! We are not in shalom.

The Anglican Report *Faith in the City* of 1985 was a call for action by Church and Nation. It opened with the words:

> A serious situation has developed in the major cities of this country . . . All the signs are that, by a vicious circle of causes and effects, the decline of the quality of life in what has been designated as 'Urban Priority Areas' is continuing, as the collapse of the West Midlands' industrial base clearly illustrates.[3]

I do not want to elaborate. Much has now been written and said about the plight of the inner cities. My book *Signs in the City* gives both the indication of non-shalom and the indications of the possibility of shalom. I only want to attest that all is not well with our nation where affluence and poverty co-exist, where those with power do not live alongside the powerless, where there is a deep-seated sense of hurt and frustration.

I would rather point to some ways by which we can move towards an understanding of a national shalom:

● *By developing an understanding attitude.* Watching TV with perception rather than prejudice, reading newspapers for information rather than entertainment, and acknowledging that God has called us to accept each other on this tiny island.

● *By looking and listening for ourselves.* Urban trails have opened the eyes and ears of many Christians as they have walked (and not driven!) through unknown streets, absorbing and feeling the realities.

● *By crossing the lines.* Living in a different area, struggling to grasp a different culture, standing where others stand – this has happened to many people who have deliberately chosen to live in difficult and demanding situations.

● *By praying with feeling – and for shalom.* A twinning arrangement will encourage the traffic of needs and hopes. A regular telephone 'hook-in' will bring realism and up-to-dateness to congregational feeling. Messengers between churches and areas will carry news and encouragement.

Unless there is a return to God's pattern and an open desire for shalom in our nation, which is built upon the foundations of justice and righteousness, judgement will follow. The Old Testament prophets knew that. For Christians, the words of Peter to the church in Caesarea put national shalom on a different plane,

> You know the message he sent to the people of Israel, proclaiming the Good News of **peace** through Jesus Christ, who is Lord of all. (Acts 10:36)

For us the shalom person who is to be 'Lord of all' calls into being the shalom community who must carry the shalom gospel to the whole nation. We know the message. We have received the Good News. We acknowledge that he is 'Lord of all'. The practical working out of the implications of this knowledge and gift will be the grounds for judgement. It is those who do the word of God rather than those who merely hear it who are commended. The credal statement 'Jesus is Lord' is the starting point, not the finishing tape. Faith without actions is dead.

Therefore where and how we live, the decisions we take, the attitudes we carry and the response we make as Christians committed to shalom will reach into every aspect of our lives. Financial management, political involvement, educational opportunity, and fairness in living standards are all part of the package.

In working towards shalom within our own nation we take on a threefold responsibility – prophet, priest and king. As prophets of shalom we are to continually remind ourselves and our nation that we are answerable to God for the way we live and the consequence of our life style on others – whether that be stewardship of resources or the implications of decisions. As priests of shalom we are to embody and demonstrate both the all-embracing reaching out of God's love and desire for human wholeness and the consequence of that in our own inner harmony and healing. As kings of shalom we are to have responsible domain over all and, like the kings of the Old Testament, our ruling must be for the sake of others with a special care for justice and compassion for the alienated and dispossessed.

Between Nations

The cosmopolitan complexity of our cities, the multi-faith dimension of religion, and the multi-culture of the ethnic minorities have brought the world and its tensions to our own nation. We have come a long way from the idea of a single race state. The apparent simplicity of a small nation struggling for survival in the Old Testament days is illustrated in the letter Solomon wrote to Hiram of Tyre:

Because of the constant wars my father David had to fight against the enemy countries all round him, he could not build a temple for the worship of the Lord his God until the Lord had given him victory over all his enemies. But now the Lord my God has given me **peace** on all my borders.(1 Kgs 5:3–4)

This clearly implies that shalom cannot exist alongside warfare, is connected with the presence of God himself and must spill over from national experience to border relationships.

The idea that frontiers require the spreading shalom is picked up in the Psalms where after the return of the exiles and the restoration of the city of God the people sing of the God who

Keeps your borders **safe**. (Ps 147:14)

Those who work for shalom between the nations have an honoured place, even in their failure.

The ambassadors who tried to bring about **peace** are crying bitterly. (Is 33:7)

Jesus himself refers to peace between the nations in the parable about the cost of discipleship where he tells of one king who

Will send messengers to meet the other king to ask for terms of **peace** while he is still a long way off. (Lk 14:32)

In our own day Ben Gurion, the former leader of Israel, once said:

As for security, military defensible borders, while desirable, cannot by themselves guarantee our future. Real peace with our Arab neighbours, mutual trust, and friendship: that is the only true security.

'Real peace . . . mutual trust . . . friendship . . . true security' are some key elements in shalom. But, in themselves, they are not enough.

Peacemaking (as we have seen) is much more than the absence of conflict. Peacemakers are after a new world, not the continuation of the world; they want the removal of frontiers, not their policing; and they are gripped by the one dream even as they work in a world of struggle and hurt.

One goal of the shalom-maker is to transform the political system and the people who operate it so that a state will arise which does aim at shalom justice.[4]

That is why our Church Meeting in East London passed a resolution:

WE CHRISTIANS of The Memorial Baptist Church, Plaistow BELIEVE that God's Peace on earth is violated so long as the nuclear powers: deploy weapons of mass destruction; encourage their peoples to think of each other as enemies; exchange propaganda which obscures truth and sustains tension; put self-protection above the needs of the Third World.

The continued threat of nuclear weapons is morally unacceptable. As Christians, as Peacemakers, we call upon the governments of NATO and the Warsaw Pact to:
make progressive agreements to disarm; take unilateral steps to create mutual trust.
We call upon the British Government to take a positive initiative towards peace now by cancelling its plans for Trident and Cruise missiles.

In this place of worship we will pray regularly for peace – the Peace which God gives the world in Jesus Christ. AMEN.

JUNE 1984

There are now at least two levels of making peace between the nations.

Alongside the traditional geographic, frontier tensions rooted in territorial control have grown up the increasing complex national or racial hostilities imported to another nation.

East London has faced wave after wave of incoming peoples who, while bringing the positive features of their culture, have often carried their own historical feuds or enmities. In recent years Indians have vied with Pakistanis and Tamils with Sinhalese from Sri Lanka.

The world is with us. Peacemaking for us is now much more local and more personal.

Television has brought an immediacy of knowledge to what was once a distant and remote world – we are now in a global village. Population mobility across the frontiers has introduced us to different cultures and religions – whether we be tourists going abroad or inner city people living alongside the immigrant. Awareness of environmental and ecological issues brings us face-to-face with acid rain or soil erosion, nuclear waste dumping or the loss of the rain forests – and all the time we are compelled to recognise that we are one world.

Economically, the simple categories of the past are finished – the idea of a First World (more developed), a Second World (centrally planned) and a Third World (less developed) is out of date. The world has become a single, interdependent, interacting, global manufacturing system which cuts across old notions of nation-status or groups of countries.

At the Wheaton Conference in 1983 on the Nature and Mission of the Church the word 'transformation' surfaced as a preferable alternative to the term development. The reasons given were that the word development implies that poverty is the result of Third World ignorance rather than oppressive and unjust economic structures. Transformation underlines the need to change the system and to be applied to rich and poor alike. So *Transformation* became the title of a new journal 'dedicated to conservation of all that meets biblical standards of truth, righteousness, justice and shalom. And to transformation of all that does not'.

Sometimes the welter of words and the proliferation of causes blind us to the simple truth. We need to see it all through the eyes of a child. When a wet day in Oslo drove us into the International Children's Museum we found a display of paintings, music, dolls and toys from across the world. For some reason, Ireland and Thailand had been placed together and in the centre of that section I found this, written by a boy, aged 14 years, from Thailand, beside a picture of warfare:

What I see about the world now is that people all over the world are becoming more and more selfish. They fight in order to make themselves great. There are wars here and there. The world has become an unpleasant place to live in. The land is covered with blood. Millions of people are suffering from wars. The number of deaths becomes more and more.

I would like to beg all countries that are making war – stop what you are doing. Why don't we live peacefully instead of making wars? I have long wished that our world were not like the picture I am drawing now!

The Whole Earth

It is, of course, part of the Bible dream that God will reign over the whole earth. National shalom, peace on the borders and the removal of racial and cultural barriers are part of the process that must lead to the universal shalom.

The Old Testament begins the chorus:

> How wonderful it is to see a messenger coming across the mountains, bringing good news, the news of **peace**! (Is 52:7)

This expected messenger – Messiah is the shalom servant of whom Isaiah said:

> But now many nations will marvel at him, and kings will be speechless with amazement. They will see and understand something they had never known. (Is 52:15)

This world 'shalom' will begin on the landbridge that joins Asia to Africa and Europe. This promised ruler will come from Bethlehem:

> When he comes, he will rule his people with the strength that comes from the Lord and with the majesty of the Lord God himself. His people will live in **safety** because people all over the earth will acknowledge his greatness, and he will bring peace. (Mic 5:4–5)

And the fulfilment of this is in the one of whom they sang

> Glory to God in the highest heaven, and **peace** on earth to those with whom he is pleased! (Lk 2:14)

and who, entering the city of Jerusalem on Palm Sunday
fulfilled the prophecy of Zechariah:

> Look your king is coming to you!
> He comes triumphant and victorious,
> but humble and riding on a donkey –
> on a colt, the foal of a donkey . . .
> Your king will make **peace** among the nations;
> he will rule from sea to sea. (Zech 9:9–10)

But it is left to Paul to most clearly set out the Christian belief
that follows from the credal cry 'Jesus is Lord':

> Through the Son, then, God decided to bring the whole
> universe back to himself. God **made peace** through his
> Son's death on the cross, and so brought back to himself all
> things, both on earth and in heaven. (Col 1:20)

And here the redemptive act of God reaches out in a finale of
shalom that covers all creation – in time and eternity. Shalom
embraces all.

All this lies behind the activity and attitudes of Christians.
They will obey the mandate of Matthew chapter 28 'to go into
all the world and preach the Gospel'. They will put Psalm 24,
'The earth is the Lord's', alongside the more personal Psalm
23. They will be involved in the World Development Movement, be concerned about One World Week, know about
Amnesty, be watchful on conservation and understanding
about ecology.

When two of our church members completed their missionary training they came back to us for a service of commissioning and valediction before going to Nepal. Their request for
the service was that we sing with, and for, them the song:

> Shalom, my friends
> Shalom, my friends
> God's peace, my friends
> Go with you now
> And stay with you
> In all you do
> Shalom! Shalom!

Visually and powerfully in that service was set the shalom –
expressed in The Peace, the Communion, and the Valediction. For the world!

In this sense all Christians are members of the 'Holy,
Catholic and Apostolic Church' sharing in the Ecumenical
Movement. Whether we live in First, Second, or Third
World; whether we rejoice at or repent of past imperialism
and colonialism; whether we are part of the sending or
receiving church (and in the UK we are now both).

As the BBC announcer used to say: 'This is the World at
One'!

Shalom has a global overview. Shalom people have to get
behind the jargon of the official reports and grasp the reality.
When the United Nations World Commission on Environment and Development published *Our Common Future* in 1983
three questions were faced:

> How healthy is the world's environment?
> How can we sustain our economic growth and our social
> development without destroying our planet?
> And what can we all do to help?

The Commission looked at population explosion, world
economy, new technologies and transport systems – and all
the ways that global ecology and human development
interact. The report ended on this note

> We are serving notice – an urgent notice based on the latest
> and best scientific evidence – that the time has come to take
> the decisions needed to secure the resources to sustain this
> and coming generations.

Much has been done since 1983 in the field of environment –
and in nuclear disarmament and awareness of world poverty.

But we have a long way to go. During one week in the
autumn of 1987 I journeyed from Israel back to East London
and then on to Belfast. In Israel we had seen the city of
shalom, Jerusalem, split into Jewish, Christian, Armenian
and Muslim quarters and sensed the underlying, simmering
hostilities. In East London we stepped back into the cauldron

of change made from the unemployment and poverty stemming from industrial run down, sharpened by the polarisation created by the new Docklands Development where yuppie affluence sat uneasily beside the struggle of the Eastenders and fanned by the prejudice and 'scapegoating' on all sides of the racial divide. In Belfast we saw for ourselves the physical starkness of corrugated iron and barbed wire together with the rash of graffiti that graphically portrayed history and hurt. Taken together the three cities presented an overwhelming picture of ingrained division, continuing hostility and a bleak future.

Yet that was not the whole picture. In Belfast we talked with Protestant and Catholic consultants at the Royal Victoria Hospital – and ended in prayer; we visited new centres like the Bridge Project built to carry the message of shalom through the Urban Mission Trust. In East London we know hundreds of men and women who refuse to withdraw from the struggle and strive for the shalom of the city. And in Israel we walked through Manger Square in Bethlehem, stooping under the lintel that led into the crypt beneath the Church of Nativity where the birth of the Prince of shalom is celebrated.

We have not yet arrived, but we are on the journey. We are living towards the vision. Around us the whole of creation groans in the travails of pregnancy (Rom 8:19–22) but we believe that, like the exiled people of the Bible, we

Will be led out of the city in **peace**
The mountains and hills will burst into singing
and the trees will shout for joy. (Is 55:12)

For shalom will be, and it will be universal, for all people and for all creation.

Shalom – the welfare in which all material and spiritual well-being
is comprehended; health, welfare, security, tranquillity . . .
whether for individual or for society, shalom is the harmonious co-
operation of all human forces towards ethical and spiritual ends
which men call the Kingdom of God.

A Jewish commentary on Numbers 6:26

Foundations

If we will have peace without a worm in it, lay we the foundations of justice and righteousness.

Oliver Cromwell

God has already placed Jesus Christ as the one and only foundation, and no other foundation can be laid.

1 Cor 3:11

The Necessity

I have been concerned in the building of two large community centres and each time I have been astonished at the extensive work required for the foundations. Upon them rests the whole structure. They must be strong enough to resist the under-mining water, the threat of earth tremor, the weight of the floor above and the corrosion of time. Foundations are hidden, but crucial. They are primary, preceding and supporting all else.

The parable about the two house builders told by Jesus (Mt 7:24–26) underlines the importance of building on rock as, in a storm, one house stands and the other collapses. It is echoed by Paul when he writes about building on the 'one and only foundation.' (1 Cor 3:10–15)

This book now moves to the practice, or process, of shalom. We have sketched out the human search portrayed in greetings, haunting our dreams and reaching out to the authenticity of shalom within the realities of human existence. We have set out the pattern of shalom as a gift of God that is to be rooted in us; made personal, for sharing and to become universal. Now we check out the way to enter, continue and end in shalom. The process, or building, of shalom, begins with the right foundation, moves on in time through continuation and culminates in a personal and social consummation.

False Foundations

False foundations are fundamentally dangerous, but superficially attractive. They are quicker and cheaper and, usefully, hidden. Judgement comes later, when the original builders have moved on, or under the stress of great pressures, when no one can help. This is confirmed in our human experience – beneath many individual and community disasters lie the faults and failures of an inadequate foundation. Wholeness collapses and well-being is not sustained. A facade of falseness masks the inner reality of inadequate foundations.

The dangers of 'false shalom' are a constant prophetic theme. Those who fail to dig deep, rely on the wrong material, or gloss over the realities do others a major disservice. They say 'all is well' (shalom) when all is not well. They lull their listeners into a counterfeit sense of security and they have compromised their message and themselves. There is therefore bitter controversy between the true and the false prophets which centres around the nature of shalom – whether it is 'peace at any price' or harmony built solidly on justice for all. Ezekiel attacks the prophets who have failed the people:

> The prophets mislead my people by saying **all is well**. All is certainly not well! (Ezek 13:10, cf. 13:16)

Jeremiah sees the superficiality of approach and the refusal to face up to the hurt of a nation that is a consequence of social sin:

> They act as if my people's wounds were only scratches. '**All is well**', they say, when all is not well. (Jer 8:11)

In a passage denouncing Israel's leaders Micah counters the prevailing philosophy that money can buy anything:

> My people are deceived by prophets who promise **peace** to those who pay them, but threaten war to those who don't. (Mic 3:5)

All three prophets use the word shalom. They recognise the widespread yearning for well-being, wholeness and harmony that is God's purpose for individuals and communities. But they make it quite plain that this shalom is not possible, and certainly will not last, if human beings build on false foundations. In this conflict, continually renewed through the centuries, the catchword upon which everything turns is shalom. For the true prophet, there can be no shalom if things are not as they ought to be.

Those who tell people what they want to hear rather than the truth they need to hear; those who ignore the ticking timebomb of a dishonest legal system; those who duck the responsibilities of public leadership, secular or religious; all are guilty of creating suspect, and ultimately destructive, social structures.

Even when human beings cloak their efforts with a religious veneer; even when worship is loud and lively; and even when special and specific offerings are made for the purpose of shalom – nothing will last and nothing will stand unless the deeper, God-designed requirements are built into the very base of human life and society. In a bible picture, it is no use whitewashing a wall which is about to collapse. That is what Amos underscores.

> The Lord says, 'I hate your religious festivals; I cannot stand them! When you bring **burnt-offerings** and grain-offerings I will not accept them . . . Stop your noisy songs; I do not want to listen to your harps. Instead, let justice flow like a stream and righteousness like a river that never goes dry'. (Amos 5:22–24)

Those who are called to be custodians of God's truth and guardians of the well-being of others carry a God-given responsibility. Like the sentry on the walls of the medieval cities they are to be concerned for the safety and welfare of the community and can only cry out 'all is well' when no dangers threaten. But danger comes from within as well as from the outside and the people of God have to probe deeply to ensure that the real foundations for shalom are in place. Just as war marks the outward absence of shalom between nations, injustice is the measure of the absence of shalom within society.

The making of peace is hard work because we are talking about basic changes in the way we order our lives – and that has to do with power. Shalom is created by and requires intervention that will redistribute power. That means justice – and doing right (righteousness). Since that is the nature of God that must be the characteristic of God's people – and God's world.

Real Foundations

Justice and righteousness, these are the only possible foundations for a society striving for shalom – and for the individual wanting 'peace with God'. Shalom cannot survive in conditions of injustice and unrighteousness, whether that be social or personal. That is made clear in the name given to the city of God. Jeru-shalom means 'foundations of shalom'.

Bring Forth Justice[1] by Waldron Scott has been called the best evangelical statement of the integral relationship between mission, discipleship and social justice. The triangular relationship is part of the bedrock of true shalom. God's people are called to a faithful and obedient response to the God who demands justice, who justifies men and women by faith in his Son and who sends them forth in the power of his Spirit to work for justice in all the nations. The book is not the product of detached scholarship. It was written by a missionary veteran with 25 years service and is a passionate, biblical, holistic, six-continent interpretation of the Christian mission in the context of an oppressed world.

What others have said in their own writing about the world I want to affirm about my own country and mission within it. We cannot isolate components. Discipleship is not worked out in a vacuum. Mission is not limited to the verbal. Justice has to do with relationships. All are bound together and underneath the malaise and impotence of Christian life in the UK is the failure to understand this. That is especially true in the urban areas and the attitudes towards them. We have been selective in our theology and partial in the Gospel – much about the church, little about the kingdom; a concern for the external and an evasion of reality.

That is why, in the New Testament, Paul writes sharply about the way Christians can become preoccupied with side issues and miss the real point. So when the early church argues about the eating of meat (even on a religious, idolatrous level) Paul lifts the debate to another dimension:

> God's Kingdom is not a matter of eating and drinking, but of the righteousness, **peace**, and joy which the Holy Spirit gives. (Rom 14:17)

Here are put together the foundation (righteousness) and the consequence (joy) of the central theme of shalom, which is to be the gift of God.

And all this is focused and embodied in the person and the work of Jesus Christ, who alone can make us right with God.

> For Christ Himself has brought us **peace** by making Jews and Gentiles one people . . . To create out of the two races one new people in union with himself, in this way making peace. (Eph 2:14–15)

The one who is the founder of Christianity is the foundation stone. He has brought into being and inaugurated a new era, gathering into himself the Old Testament hopes and convictions and providing in himself the enabling and enduring bedrock for all who follow him.

In him come together the Nazareth Manifesto (Lk 4:16–21) with its emphasis on justice (the poor, captive, blind and oppressed) and the Galilean Mandate (Mt 28:16–20) with its stress on discipleship (baptise, teach and obey). It is through him, the shalom person, that we understand and enter into the shalom community of faith.

> Now that we have been put right with God through faith, we have **peace** with God through our Lord Jesus Christ. (Rom 5:1)

The ministry of Jesus between Nazareth and Galilee was the establishment of community between those who were excluded and those who excluded them. His acts of healing the sick, forgiving the guilty, raising the dead, and feeding the hungry are all actions that re-establish God's will for shalom in a world grown chaotic through self-centredness.

The continuing ministry of his people goes on from that foundation. We are to go to the world with that constant concern for the well-being and salvation of all which is shalom. If we are to do God's word as well as talk about it, we need a vision to guide our doing and acting. That vision is shalom which is embodied in Jesus. That shalom grows from, and depends upon, justice and doing right.

Righteousness and Justice

We have separated the ideas but the Bible has married them together. Again and again the two words appear together as a single phrase or in the same sentence. Social justice and personal righteousness hold together. These are the foundations of shalom.

> I myself will teach your people, and give them prosperity and **peace**. Justice and right will make you strong. (Is 54:13–14)

This is the nature of God himself. Doing that which is right, being just. What he is he expects from his creation. If individuals do not live rightly and if there is injustice within society then the order and harmony of shalom breaks down. The doing of righteousness and justice results in the building of the community of shalom in which the oppressed and disenfranchised have dignity and power. Failure here leads to injustice and alienation which ends in turmoil and anxiety with no chance of well-being and peace.

God has communicated his righteous-justice to mankind. His concern for right relationships between himself and between people is set out in teaching like the Ten Commandments. The prophets and the psalmists preach and sing about the strength and beauty of right living and just behaviour. Jesus comes calling disciples to have the right attitude to God and man and to live and to act in accordance with this. The kingdom of God means doing what God wants – and that means personal 'rightness' and social togetherness under the rule of the living God. This is not an irrelevant, other-worldly philosophy, it is a startling, down-to-earth truth that speaks sharply to today's world.

On the very day that the Brixton riots in 1980 erupted 200 people met in St Martins-in-the-Bullring, Birmingham, to launch the Evangelical Coalition for Urban Mission. Looking at injustice in our society, recognising our own imperfections and blindnesses, and increasingly aware of God's desire for shalom we drew up a Manifesto which included:

> We must actively express God's demands for love, justice and reconciliation throughout society and for liberation of all people from every form of oppression.[2]

Those of us who live and work in the inner cities of the UK know that the shalom which is God's purpose for all must be rooted and grounded in righteousness – justice. That is why in Newham, the London Borough in which I have lived for over 20 years, you will see a United Reformed Church set in a densely populated multi-racial district changing its name to Shalom Centre and openly placarding their concern for justice and peace. That is why Roger Sainsbury, a leader in the neighbouring evangelical Mayflower Family Centre could write after his work in Liverpool and East London a book with the unexpected title of *Justice on the Agenda*.

That is why under the headline 'Only the tree of justice will produce fruits of peace' a letter in the *Methodist Recorder* from Vic Watson in Walworth, South London followed the Tottenham and Brixton disorders in 1985 and said:

> We are tired of listening to politicians of all parties who seem to be more interested in gaining political points than in a genuine concern for people who are constantly being damaged and battered.
>
> Their words will always sound hollow and hypocritical until they can demonstrate their care by coming together with a united plan of action to alleviate the scandal of inner city deprivation.
>
> This inner-city, multi-racial congregation pleads for the planting of trees of justice; for some immediate signs that those whom we elect to work for the 'general good' really do care.

'Rights' has become a contemporary word. 'Human rights' has swung to 'I know my rights' but the full Christian will be as concerned for the rights of others as he/she is for their own and, above all, wrestle for the right pattern of relationships that God requires. This is to be worked out at the personal level of 'righteousness by faith' as well as the wider justice in the community and the two are inseparable. 'Those whom God has joined together let no man put asunder!'

If we ignore this in our own country the message will come over more loudly from our Christian brothers and sisters in the Third World. It was his experience of the Philippines that caused Perry Yoder to write his book *Shalom: The Bible's Word for Salvation, Justice, and Peace* and to say:

> The major thesis of this book is that shalom, biblical peace, is squarely against injustice and oppression . . . Shalom demands a transforming of unjust social and economic orders.[3]

Nowhere does the Old Testament tradition make a separation between the 'social' and the 'spiritual' of the kind to which we have become accustomed in the modern western world. Such a division is in fact quite alien to biblical thought . . . The spirituality of the Old Testament writers is a justice spirituality, in marked contrast to the false division between issues considered as spiritual and those considered social or political. Union and communion with God cannot be achieved apart from the achievement of earthly justice and shalom, peace, and this peace is not compatible with wickedness (Isa. 48.22). On the contrary, the breaking of the covenant with God has consequences which are earthly and material: a broken covenant leads to a broken and devastated earth (Isa. 24).[4]

Kenneth Leech

Continuation

All our works begun, continued, and ended in thee.
Book of Common Prayer

Peace is a daily, a weekly, a monthly process, gradually changing opinions, slowly eroding old barriers, quietly building new structures.[1]
John F. Kennedy

The two key words for those who want to continue in the way of shalom are covenant and consequences. Covenant holds together the binding relationships between a human being and the Creator and the parallel solidarity with others. The consequences that flow from the covenant reach into every aspect of life.

Keeping the Covenant

We use the word in everyday living. Students are encouraged and supported by their parents through a deed of covenant which is a financial agreement between parents and child (and the tax inspector!). In the world of building we find a 'restrictive covenant' and when couples get married in our churches they enter into the covenant of marriage.

But these are only contemporary echoes of a biblical shout. What the word covenant means today and what it ought to mean can be expressed in a series of couplets which indicate how far we have watered down and weakened the covenant theme.

a promise	a binding commitment
legal framework	a loving relationship
external	internal
only for time	eternal
collective	deeply personal
individual	corporate
business	set in worship

In this word, as with many others, we have weakened, cheapened, and humanised the strong, powerful, God-given themes.

The unfolding of God's covenant with his people progresses from Noah with the rainbow as the sign of the promise God makes 'to all living beings' (Gen 9:8–17); through Abraham with circumcision as the sign and emphasis on faith and obedience (Gen 15 and 17); into the Sinai covenant drawing together God's commands and the response from the people of God.

> If you will obey me and keep my covenant, you will be my own people. The whole earth is mine, but you will be my chosen people, a people dedicated to me alone, and you will serve me as priests. (Ex 19:5)

It is the undergirding theme of the whole of the Old Testament or Covenant and is fully realised and powerfully set out by Jesus who comes to inaugurate the New Covenant. He restores the original purpose, embodies it in himself and makes it universal.

Into the covenant Christians enter. It is already present and we are the latest arrivals. It is God's gift to which we respond. Because of our failure in understanding and obedience we renew our promises at the communion service or in an Annual Covenant Service.

We are chosen and called to live in covenant-faithfulness. This is expressed in our love towards God and neighbour. All that the Bible speaks about in the blessing of God, the freedom of the community exhibiting the harmony of shalom, the concern for the deprived and the handicapped are held together by the theme of covenant. Within this the people of God walk, without this they cannot continue.

Shalom must always be the result of the covenant. Whether it be at the level of human relationship:

> Early next morning each man made his promise and sealed it with a vow. Isaac said goodbye to them, and they parted as **friends**. (Gen 26:31)

Or in the God-ward aspect:

> Then Jonathan said to David, '**God be with you**. The Lord will make sure that you and I, and your descendants and mine, will for ever keep the sacred promise we have made to each other'. (1 Sam 20:42)

The two words are inseparable. Where there is a full working out of the covenant principle there is the shalom community.

> The connection between the two words is so strong that in this context shalom seems to hvae become a kind of official term. The thought may be that the relationship of shalom is sealed by both parties in a covenant. Conversely, it may be that the covenant inaugurates a relationship of shalom.

The highpoint of the relationship between covenant and shalom is reached by the prophets. Again and again human fulfilment and God's presence are linked together in the 'covenant of peace':

> I will keep for ever my promise of **peace**. (Is 54:10)

> I will make a covenant with them that guarantees their **security**. (Ezek 34:25)

> In my covenant I promised them life and **well-being**, and this is what I gave them . . . They lived in **harmony** with me; they not only did what was right themselves, but they also helped many others to stop doing evil. (Mal 2:5–6)

But since no one can do God's work without God's Spirit, not even God's Son, there is a close inter-connection between covenant, shalom and the Holy Spirit. It is the indwelling Spirit who enables those in the new covenant to enter into the life of shalom whether that be expressed in the language of the hymn 'Join each to each, and all to thine' or the words of Scripture

> To be controlled by the Spirit results in life and **peace**. (Rom 8:6)

Only those with a renewed understanding of the Covenant will be able to continue in the way of shalom. Without this framework, and the partnership of the Holy Spirit, shalom remains an unfulfilled dream. But when the covenant-people know the power of the Spirit then shalom becomes a consequence in personal life style, in the shalom community and in the wider world.

Consequence 1: Personal Life Style

Within the scaffolding of the covenant springs up a new pattern of relationships and attitudes. Christians are urged to offer their lives in God's service and to:

> Do everything possible on your part to live in **peace** with everybody. (Rom 12:18)

This is no easy option. It will involve effort – or striving; it has to do with living; and it is to be a reflection in time of the nature of God himself:

> Strive for perfection; listen to my appeals; agree with one another; live in **peace**. And the God of love and **peace** will be with you. (2 Cor 13:11)

The shalom life style is expressed within personal relationships, the use of possessions (especially money) and through the ministry of reconciliation (being a peacemaker). Woven together, these produce a tapestry of shalom that is visible, tangible and is a consequence of the spiritual wisdom that is rooted in the covenant.

Shalom within personal relationships is far more than a vague benevolence. It is specific and definite. Written into the marriage covenant, carried within family life, developed in friendships, and worked out in community living it reaches into every experience of human 'togetherness'. It is the touchstone and guideline in difficulties and the purpose and goal of all human partnerships.

Even in the difficult matter of a marriage between a believer and an unbeliever – and the question of separation – the key is shalom.

God has called you to live in **peace**. (1 Cor 7:15)

This 'living in peace' applies at all levels. The wholeness or well-being that is shalom will be seen positively in the accepting, open, direct, caring and continuing love for the other that wills the best. The negative, non-shalom features of backbiting, suspicions, moodiness, fault-finding, are to drop away through what John Oman called 'the expulsive power of a new affection'.

In practical terms this will mean a sustained effort to work at those things that promote harmony and to eradicate those that destroy. In this, the understanding of body language (how people sit, use their hands, direct their eyes) and the development of an empathy of understanding that reads the indications of dis-ease and a bridge-building attitude that refuses to allow gaps of communication to persist are all essential.

No one is born with all the social skills and none have fully arrived. Relationships have to be worked at, wrestled with and not taken for granted or allowed to stagnate. It is a continuing process.

Two books stand together on my bookshelf. Both are about life style and both were written in the early 1980s. One is rooted in a British movement, the other grew from an international dimension. Yet the first opens with a global statement and the second ends with a personal commitment.

Life Style. A parable of sharing by A. H. Dammer begins with a world perspective:

1. The resources of the Earth for sustaining the development of the growing Human Family are not inexhaustible and

therefore have to be conserved for our own and for
future generations.

2. The distribution of these resources among the members
   of the Human Family is grossly inequitable. They have
   to be distributed more fairly.

3. To enable a more equitable distribution of these
   resources and their necessary conservation, those who
   are at present consuming inordinately or even substan-
   tially more than their share have to consume less; in
   other words, 'to live more simply that all of us may
   simply live'.[3]

An Evangelical Commitment to Simple Life-Style closes 30 tightly
argued pages with 'Our Resolve':

So then, having been freed by the sacrifice of our Lord
Jesus Christ, in obedience to his call, in heart-felt
compassion for the poor, in concern for evangelism,
development and justice, and in solemn anticipation of the
Day of Judgement, we humbly commit ourselves to
develop a just and simple life-style, to support one another
in it and to encourage others to join us in this commitment.

We know that we shall need time to work out its implications and that the task will not be easy. May Almighty
God give us his grace to be faithful! Amen.[4]

Together, the books face head-on the Christian response to
possessions, especially money. Since shalom has to do with
personal, corporate and universal wholeness and harmony
and since key issues like affluence, poverty, development,
power and justice are skewered together in the shalom agenda
the life style of the individual must hold together belief and
behaviour. What we do is a visible expression of what we
believe. A concern for others, a caring life and a commitment
to shalom will lead to simplicity, sharing and stewardship.
Simplicity is the personal style, sharing is the corporate
expression and stewardship is the accountability to God.

Simplicity in style surfaces in many forms. The clothes we
wear, the furniture we buy, the style of our car, the food we
eat, the appropriateness of our housing scale and our leisure

costs all make up a picture that reflects ostentation or simplicity.

Sharing of resources with others spans church buildings and equipment, car usage and house ownership, the passing on of clothes and a watch-over concern for other children.

Stewardship is accountability to God for what we do with what we have. It covers all that which we call our own – time, possessions, resources and skills. These we hold in trust, and are answerable to God for our use of them.

Shalom people are reconcilers, peacemakers. They draw their mandate from the words of Jesus in the Beatitudes.

> Happy are those who work for **peace**. God will call them his children! (Mt 5:9)

and see their example in the life of Jesus, the Prince of peace. This is far more than a resistance to war. It is that, but much more. Even movements like the Fellowship of Reconciliation, which came into being in 1914, as a direct consequence of a pledge between a German Lutheran and a British Quaker now say:

> We're a Fellowship instead of a movement or organisation because we believe peace is about individuals just as much as countries, about all people enjoying just and peaceful relationships. You cannot separate personal, inner peace from peace between nations or vice versa.

The famous Prayer for Peace began to circulate in 1981 in England. Its source is not known, and it has no ties with any single denomination or faith. Within months of its appearance it had been adopted by many community and religious leaders and their organisations. Within less than six months its worldwide circulation was announced by Mother Teresa of Calcutta. Just nine months later the Prayer was said by the 900 delegates at the Assembly of World Religions – probably the first time the world's leading religions have ever prayed together the one prayer. It was translated into many languages and clearly reflected the yearning of many people. I hung the prayer at three points within Lawrence Hall, the community centre where I worked, and received many requests for the words:

> Lead me from death to life, from falsehood to truth
> Lead me from despair to hope, from fear to trust
> Lead me from hate to love, from war to peace
> Let peace fill our heart, our world, our universe.
> Peace.   Peace.   Peace.

In this continuing pilgrimage from the world that is anti-shalom into the world that is shalom prayer is the factor that changes attitudes. Whether that be prayer shared in a group, linked in a worldwide exercise or a solo voice – it is the power that changes and allows the continuation of shalom.

This attitude is positive rather than negative. As one Wayside Poster used to say: 'Peace is not the absence of war, it is the presence of love'. And, even more powerfully, the words of Walter Knight which became the slogan of the Baptist Peace Fellowship of North America:

> Peace plans its strategy and encircles the enemy.
> Peace marshals its forces and storms the gates.
> Peace gathers its weapons and pierces the defence.
> Peace, like war, is waged.
> But Christ has turned it all around:
> the weapons of peace are love, joy, goodness, long suffering
> the arms of peace are justice, truth, patience, prayer.
> the strategy of peace brings safety, welfare, happiness
> the forces of peace are the sons and daughters of God.

The attitude, and life style, expressed in both prayers is rooted in our faith in Jesus Christ, who is our Peace, in whom God is reconciling the world and through whom God calls us to the ministry of peacemaking.

Peace or shalom is not only our goal, but our means. The foundation of shalom is justice. The force of shalom is love.

Although this personal life style is for all it is particularly relevant to, and necessary within, the inner cities of the UK. In a society that is divided, pluralistic, damaged and often bitter the shalom life style speaks of hope and wholeness. In areas of deprivation and poverty the emergence of caring and sharing individuals operating as stewards of resources and reconcilers in relationships points on to the shalom purpose and dream of God.

Consequence 2: In the Shalom Community

Life style is not worked out in a vacuum and the shalom person must be part of the shalom community. Isolation has no part in shalom. The past 20 years have seen a renewal of cell and congregational life that has allowed and encouraged the continuation of shalom in a wide variety of forms.

In the London Borough of Newham the Shalom Justice and Peace Centre introduces itself as 'A centre for action and reflection on justice and peace, including employment action projects, a neighbourhood centre, and a worship and reflection centre. Shalom is a biblical word which describes peace and wholeness in individual and community life'. Across the River Thames in Balham the Shalom Community Youth Ministries 'is an interdenominational, evangelical and multiracial outreach with the purpose of presenting the Good News of the Lord Jesus Christ to young people living in the Inner City areas, with the result that young people develop themselves as whole persons according to the capacities God has given them'.

In 1987, I was invited by the Urban Mission Trust to share in the celebration of the opening of The Bridge in Belfast. The Bridge Centre is to be found alongside the off-licence, launderette, carry-out, pubs and shops on the lower Ravenhill Road. The converted three-storey building 'is an attempt to establish a visible Christian presence at street level, where people can see, hear and experience for themselves the Good News of God's kingdom'.

All these are part of a massive wave that is sweeping through our institutional break-waters and stirring up our ecclesiastical beaches! On one side the National Association of Community Centres and Networks shows the diversity of this continuing shalom activity. On the other side, the presence of more than 400 new congregations since 1970 in inner London alone reveals the scale. David Wilcox, a minister from Abingdon, on sabbatical leave in Newham described the shalom communities.

> Inevitably I came with certain expectations of the area and of the churches. I had read *Faith in the City* and I was prepared for all the indications of deprivation. And I came expecting to find the churches small, struggling and depressed.
>
> But I have found a tremendous vitality. Many evangelical churches and Christian fellowships are flourishing – not large, but with a mood of hope and purpose as they seek to witness to Christ and serve the community. There is an exciting growing together of white and black-led churches. I attended a united prayer meeting where black pastors gave moving expression to the spirit of reconciliation at work – and what vibrancy they brought to the worship!
>
> All over Newham there is a growing network of church centres offering facilities and care to the community.
>
> Do you recall how Isaiah 35 speaks of flowers blossoming in the wilderness, streams of water flowing through the desert? I have seen the blossom, I have seen the stream. There is New Life in Newham.

These shalom communities build their agendas around three focal points: worship that is lively, participatory and relevant; fellowship that is real, loving and involved; proclamation that is visual and verbal. Worship is central. Strong singing, a biblical basis, many taking part and constant reference to the contemporary setting are features. Without the unifying, binding effect of worship there is atomisation and impotence. Unless there are roots in scriptural teaching and the regular observance of the Communion there is an anarchical individualism. In a chapter given over to worship Paul underlined God's purpose of shalom:

> God does not want us to be in disorder but in **harmony and peace**. (1 Cor 14:33)

Church fellowship or body-life is strong. 'The Peace' here is no formal ritual, it is all-embracing and for all. Homes are open, regular weekly 'share and care' cells are the rule, and the gifts of each member are called out. Often those engaged in local politics or specific ministries take time to share with the whole congregation. Decision-making is but one way for shalom to become real.

> The peace that Christ gives is to guide you in the decisions you make; for it is to this **peace** that God has called you together in the one body. (Col 3:15)

Proclamation is a priority. Personal evangelism and social action go hand in hand. Street demonstrations and public prayer meetings go with participation in Town Shows and door-to-door visiting. These shalom communities are on their feet and understand Paul's urging of the early church to have

> As your shoes the readiness to announce the good news of **peace**. (Eph 6:15)

There is a wholeness and harmony in this community life. Worship, fellowship and mission blend in a new realism. Shalom is tangible. Nor is this the monopoly of the new churches. Evidence of resurrection in the older, declining congregations is on all sides. One church I remembered as a formal, somewhat dreary congregation wrote an ambiguously phrased letter to me after I had visited them and glimpsed a fresh, renewing vitality under the leadership of a woman minister:

> It was a very encouraging day for us and we were delighted that you too were able to express your joy at being with us. After your departure in the evening an impromptu session of praise and prayer continued until 9.00 pm!

Continuation in shalom is only possible within, and through, the shalom community. The double-sidedness of worship – let prayer ascend and grace descend; the binding nature of fellowship and the commitment to the ongoing mission of the church are also integral and essential elements. Here is a wholeness and a harmony that feeds, draws out and deepens shalom.

Consequence 3: In the Wider World

But worship can be egocentric and irrelevant, fellowship too easily becomes limiting and proclamation is seen as an option unless the full sweep of God's purpose in and for the world is grasped:

> Through the Son, then God decided to bring the whole universe back to himself. God made **peace** through his Son's death on the cross and so brought back to himself all things, both on earth and in heaven. (Col 1:20)

No individual and no congregation is self-sufficient. They are part of a global, cosmic process which is restlessly reaching out to ever wider aspects of the whole. The church is set in the broader framework of the kingdom and all is part of the over-cell economy or purpose of God.

Many church people are into maintenance and not mission, are concerned about the church but fail to glimpse the kingdom.

> In the church business, people are concerned with church activities, religious behaviour and spiritual things. In the Kingdom business, people are concerned with Kingdom activities, all human behaviour and everything God has made, visible and invisible. Kingdom people see human affairs as saturated with spiritual meaning and Kingdom significance.
>
> Church people think about how to get people into the church; Kingdom people think about how to get the church into the world . . . far from operating in a separate sphere greatly removed from the world, the church is God's household right smack in the middle of the disordered cosmos, existing there both to show what God intends and will do

and to be the body of Christ – the presence and agency of Jesus in the world today.[5]

All around us the continuation of God's purpose of shalom can be seen. Rippling out from the personal wholeness and the social harmony we receive through our faith and our fellowship, reaching across the geographical and denominational divides, guiding through the difficulties of change and us to face other faiths; compelling us to face political realities and world issues and to confront the 'principalities and powers'.

For years I have been bothered about the social divisions in our own society whether that be inner-city/suburban, north/south or working-class/middle-class. These polarities run right through us, colouring our personal attitudes and reflected in the constituency of our churches. That is why I welcome projects like Centre Point which seeks to draw together suburban and inner city Christians:

> The plight of our inner city areas is now well documented and there is a growing conviction among suburban Christians of all denominations that something ought to be done. But what? And by whom? We feel so powerless – so we hide our impotence behind paper walls of words, committees and good intentions. But words cannot heal divisions . . . words cannot right the wrongs.

Centre Point will enable genuine concern to be translated into positive Christian action – building bridges of love and understanding, responding to the challenge of the city and countering injustice in our society. By meeting, living, worshipping, working and reflecting together shalom will grow.

At an even wider level the emergence of 'Not Strangers but Pilgrims' – an inter-church process on the nature and purpose of the church in the light of its mission – has re-kindled the dowsed hopes many of us have for a growing together of God's people. Not in the institutional, ecumenical movement sense but in the organic, living oneness of the shalom community. We move from the theological barricades and territorial frontiers as we become pilgrims together. In the autumn of 1987 I visited a Church Centre in Milton Keynes shared by an Anglican and a Baptist Church. In the 9.30 service I listened to the reading of the Swanwick declaration:

We came with different experiences and traditions, some with long ecumenical service, some for whom this is a new adventure. We are one band of pilgrims. We are old and young, women and men, black and white, lay and ordained and we travelled from the four corners of these islands to meet at Swanwick in Derbyshire. There we met, we listened, we talked, we worshipped, we prayed, we sat in silence, deeper than words. Against the background of so much suffering and sinfulness in our society we were reminded of our call to witness that God was in Chrsit reconciling the world to himself. Wc affirmed that this world with all its sin and splendour belongs to God . . . We now declare together our readiness to commit ourselves to each other under God. Our earnest desire is to become more fully, in His own time, the One Church of Christ, united in faith, communion, pastoral care and mission. Such unity is the gift of God . . . It is our conviction that, as a matter of policy at all levels and in all places, our churches must now move from co-operation to clear commitment to each other, in search of the unity for which Christ prayed, and in common evangelism and service of the world . . . Leaving behind painful memories and reaching out for what lies ahead, we press on towards the full reconciliation in Christ of all things in heaven and on earth, that God has promised in his Kingdom.

But the church world is a tiny fragment of our society. The national average of church attendance may be between 10 and 12% but where I live it has been a third of the national average for more than a century. Small groups of Christians find themselves in a maelstrom of social change. Until we can glimpse God at work in this pluralistic, shifting kaleidoscope we live a blinkered and cloistered existence.

I've lived in West Ham for 20 years. It feels a bit like living in a wash-basin with the plug out and both taps full on!

Gurgling out of the plug-hole go those who have 'made it' – buying houses in the suburbs or moving to better jobs.

One of the taps is the visibly obvious stream of common-wealth immigrants who have come here to live and work.

The other tap is the constant flow of white people arriving to live with families or friends. They come hopeful of work, seeking anonymity or to buy houses.

Exciting but exhausting!

Living with change is not always comfortable. It threatens, questions and upsets; and some changes have to be resisted.

But it is certainly never dull and there is a richness in the new ways, the different languages and the distinctive cultures.

I believe all this is part of God's purpose. He wants us to accept and value each other and to break down the barriers.

> Lord, grant me the serenity to accept the things I cannot change,
> The courage to change the things I can
> And the wisdom to know the difference.

Shalom in a society in transition means understanding and reconciliation. Many local Christians are part of a 'Conflict and Change' programme that has grown out of an understanding of our post-industrial technological society which now challenges many assumptions. Multi-racial urban communities pose new problems for education, religions, law and order and the processes of democratic representation. The family and the way in which the generations relate to each other are no longer clearly defined. In this society stresses and strains generate uncertainty. Uncertainty separates and confuses people. In all this the dream of shalom holds and directs believers into analysis and answer, under-standing action.

Nowhere is this tension felt more sharply than in the world of the immigrant and the other faiths.

The multi-faith dimension in the British Isles has visibly shattered the long-held view that Christianity is the only practical religious option for the Anglo-Saxons or Celts. The numerical presence is itself compelling – at least 800,000 Muslims, 320,000 Hindus, 300,000 Sikhs and 100,000 Buddhists (not to mention 385,000 Jews). There are now more Muslims than Methodists, more Hindus than Baptists, more Sikhs than the URC and more Buddhists than Pentecostalists!

Since the history of Christian relations with those of other faiths is for the most part a very dismal tale we will need to see whether the accepted roads of confrontation with direct evangelism or dialogue to foster co-existence can be drawn together in the continuing aim of shalom.

But even this complex world fades into the background when we walk into the minefield of politics! When the book *Faith in Politics – Which Way should Christians vote?* written by the Conservative John Gummer, the Labour Eric Heffer and the Liberal Alan Beith (all active churchmen) was launched just before the 1987 election the *Guardian* journalist, Martin Wainwright, had a field-day:

> God was comfortably established yesterday as a basically Conservative figure with strong Socialist convictions and a broadly Alliance approach to the problems of the world He made. In an outbreak of sweetness, light and other virtues perhaps unfamiliar at Westminster, three rival MPs explained how the Deity would probably vote.[6]

The reality is not so easy! The bitterness of party politics and the entrenched attitudes make most Christians back away. But if shalom is to be established we have to wrestle at local, national, an international issues taking biblical principles into contemporary realities.

That is why the agendas of our church meetings (and our bank accounts) must include:

Third World Poverty
Ecology
Nuclear Warfare
Education

Let one example carry what I'm driving at. The Christian Ecology Group introduces itself:

It's easy to feel overwhelmed by the scale of the global problems which we increasingly hear about – the arms race, the destruction of forests, damage to cropland, declining supplies of energy and other natural resources, appalling poverty. Often they seem distant, or so severe that individual action appears pointless. But there is hope. More and more people are recognising that each one of us can make a valuable response – through changing what we consume, rethinking our treatment of other people and other creatures, and choosing more productive ways of spending our time. Our efforts combine together to change the world around us.

The Christian Ecology Group was formed by Christians sharing the belief that it is our responsibility to tackle these problems and make a stand for the ideals in which we believe.

I am aware of the plethora of causes, projects and issues which can so easily submerge us but I also know that there is no 'keeping on keeping on' in shalom unless these form part of our agenda for shalom. When I look at the items before us on a national Mission Committee: Community Work, the disabled, Social Affairs, Education, Debt, Women, Aids, International Relations, Health and Healing; I am both overwhelmed and excited. Overwhelmed at the diversity and excited by the inner knowledge that these are kingdom agenda points. Political, because this deals with ultimate meaning and aims to change the present order. Social, because this means human beings organised around questions of values and life meaning. Economic, because this involves the stewardship of money and resources.

That we may be healed. A Meditation by Therese Vanier.

That oppressed people and those who oppress them may free each other . . .

That those who are handicapped and those who think they are not, may help each other . . .

That those who need someone to listen may touch the hearts of those who are too busy . . .

That the homeless may bring joy to those who open their doors reluctantly . . .

That the lonely may heal those who think they are self sufficient . . .

That the poor may melt the hearts of the rich . . .

That seekers for truth give life to those who are satisfied they have found it . . .

That the dying who do not want to die may be comforted by those who find it hard to live . . .

That prisoners may find true freedom and liberate others from fear . . .

That those who sleep on the streets share their gentleness with those who cannot understand them . . .

That the hungry tear the veil from the eyes of those who do not hunger after justice . . .

That those who live without hope cleanse the hearts of their brothers who are afraid to live . . .

That the weak confound the strong and save them . . .

That violence be overtaken by compassion . . .

That violence be absorbed by men of peace.

That violence succumb to those who are totally vulnerable . . .

That we may be healed . . .

Consummation

> *Mid toil and tribulation,*
> *And tumult of her war,*
> *She waits the consummation*
> *Of peace for evermore;*
> *Till with the vision glorious*
> *Her longing eyes are blest,*
> *And the great church victorious*
> *Shall be the church at rest.*

Samuel Johnstone

> *I make those plans and predictions **come true**.*

Isaiah 44:26

Towards the Goal

The process of shalom has its deep-rooted foundations, its continuation within time moving, pilgrim-style, towards a goal. Shalom carries a 'yet to be', an unfinished, pointing-on quality. There is a sense of purposeful journeying.

This feeling begins early on in faith. When I asked a group of young Christians at a conference to describe themselves in one word the picture that emerged was clear-cut.

Positively	Negatively
Anticipating	Burnt-out
Working	Battle-fatigued
Learning	Mixed-up
Traveller	Restless
Searching	Struggling
Exploring	
Looking	
Journeying	

Without exception each one of the under 30s used a picture-word that sketched life as a journey. A moving towards, a wanting to achieve, and a refusal to settle down – all pointed towards a culmination, conclusion and completion that has yet to be. This consummation is to be known personally, within the church, and throughout all creation.

The idea that fulfilment and final wholeness is implicit within shalom is carried in a double biblical metaphor – in the sense of a task being finished and in the numerical concept that all have come together.

The idea of a task being ended is especially clear in the Old Testament story about the rebuilding of the Temple where shalom is translated as finished. So that in the report the Persian officials sent back to Emperor Darius they refer to the process of building that starts with the foundation and continues to the completion – for which they use shalom,

> So Sheshbazzar came and laid its foundation; construction has continued from then until the present but the Temple is still not **finished** (Ezra 5:16)

and they ask for instructions about the future. But later Nehemiah records that:

> After fifty two days of work the entire wall was **finished** . . . When our enemies in the surrounding nations heard this, they realised that they had lost face, since everyone knew that the work had been done with God's help. (Neh 6:15–16)

Here is a careful linking together of 'finished . . . work . . . with God's help' as a pen-picture of shalom.

The numerical insight which portrays shalom as totality occurs when the word is translated as 'all' or 'whole':

> **All** the people of Judah have been taken away into exile.(Jer 13:19)

> They carried off a **whole** nation and sold them as slaves . . . (Amos 1:6)

There is an ugly completeness in these pictures of an entire nation, without exception, being taken into bondage. Nothing, and no one, is excluded. All are gathered together into exile.

But it is the Temple theme which is the most germane. Running right through the account is the process that is moving towards completion, even in the details.

> The stones with which the Temple was built **had been prepared** at the quarry. (1 Kgs 6:7)

> When King Solomon **finished** all the work in the Temple.(1 Kgs 7:51)

> By this time all Solomon's projects had been completed. From the laying of the foundation of the Lord's Temple to its **completion**, all the work had been successful. (2 Chron 8:16)

Here in the physical programme of building the idea of foundation, continuation and completion are held together. This is paralleled in the New Testament image of Jesus as the new Temple and his words on the cross: 'It is finished'. Building and body are created as vehicles for the presence of God.

Personal Wholeness

> Shalom is often indicative, in Old Testament usage, of a comprehensive kind of fulfilment or completion, indeed of a perfection in life and spirit which quite transcends any success which man alone, even under the best of circumstances, is able to attain.[1]

Moving towards perfection, growing towards maturity, aiming for the finishing line are all phrases suggesting direction and fulfilment. Being prepared, working together with, entering into – all shorthand for a process.

This process continues throughout life, even in the hurt. The famous picture in the book of Hebrews about finishing the race in front of a great crowd of witnesses goes on to remind us that when we are punished, it seems to us at the time something to make us sad, not glad. Later, however

Those who have been disciplined by such punishment reap the **peaceful** reward of a righteous life. (Heb 12:11)

The recent renaissance of *Pilgrim's Progress* by John Bunyan underlines afresh the age-old theme of personal pilgrimage towards a goal, whether it be expressed in the biblical metaphor of the Promised Land, Bunyan's 'Celestial City' or the more contemporary images. There is a sense in which we are being made perfect since we are continually under reconstruction, moving ever deeper into shalom.

Yet personal wholeness is the other side of the time-divide with full and ultimate shalom in the death which leads into eternal life. For our generation R.I.P. on tombstones has become hackneyed. 'Rest in peace' fails to carry the significance and power of the original meaning in which an individual finally rests in the wholeness of God's eternity.

But the Bible sees this as God's purpose for the individuals. Early on, God says to Abraham:

You yourself will live to a ripe old age, die in **peace**, and be buried (Gen 15:15)

and the message is carried on by the prophets:

Those who live good lives will find **peace** and rest in death.(Is 57:2)

Jesus embodies the theme in the Easter Day greetings which were originally addressed to the disciples and are now shared between Christians:

Peace be with you. (Jn 20:19, 21, 26)

Christian faith sings its way towards death. Whether it be the ancient

God be at my end and at my departing

or the robust hymn of Charles Wesley:

Till death Thine endless mercies seal

there is an untypical and unexpected attitude towards death which often astonishes the non-believing observer.

When Robert – a 19-year-old member of staff at Lawrence Hall and the only son of two of our church members – died from leukemia we took a vanload of young people to the funeral service. They were part of our work experience team who had worked alongside Robert, buying their crisps and coke from him in the coffee-bar and watching him move towards death. The service in the church where Robert had belonged to the Boys' Brigade and was baptised a few months before he died was packed, strong, and alive. One of the girls, a Muslim, came back in the van with a question: 'Are Christians the only people who can sing when someone dies?'

Universal Shalom

But consummation in shalom is much greater than the individual. Final and full salvation indicates future peace in the animal world (Is 11:6–8), between people (Is 11:9) and in nature (Is 2:2–4). For since shalom defines how things should be in the material worlds, in relationships, and in personal character the final consummation will cover and gather all these together. That is why shalom is translated as 'end':

> God has numbered the days of your kingdom and brought it to an **end**. (Dan 5:26)

It is seen as the completion of God's purpose for his people:

> I make those plans and predictions **come true**. (Is 44:26)

The expectation of a final state of eternal peace is a strong element in Old Testament eschatology which finds constant expression in the prophets and other writings. This widespread and many-sided expectation emerges in several forms. There is the idea of a restoration of the conditions in Paradise, the promise of international peace under divine direction, the expectation of a humble king in the last age who will bring a time of peace and a prophetic proclamation about the shalom which will cover the whole earth.

The New Testament focuses and intensifies the shalom

hope. For Christians, this universal shalom has dawned with the coming of the 'Prince of Peace'. The name tells us that the One who bears God's commission is Messiah and the guarantor and guardian of peace and the coming kingdom. Restoration, promise, expectation, vision . . . all are drawn together:

> God made **peace** through his Son's death on the cross and so brought back to himself all things both on earth and in heaven. (Col 1:20)

This coming together of all things within the kingdom of God includes the overthrow and elimination of evil in all its guises as the 'principalities and powers' are defeated:

> God, our source of **peace**, will soon crush Satan under your feet. (Rom 16:20)

In *Living toward a Vision* Walter Brueggemann argues against a theology of despair:

> Shalom is rooted in a theology of hope, in the powerful, buoyant conviction that the world can and will be transformed and renewed, that life can and will be changed and newness can and will come.[2]

Hope for the future, whether that be personal or cosmic, is not escapism. Ronald Sider, in his book *Cry Justice*,[3] lets the Bible speak for itself on the issues of hunger and poverty through a series of inter-connected Bible passages. Under the section 'Salvation completed; the Shalom for which we hope' four selected passages draw together the strands that come together in the final consummation. The themes and passages are:

The Lord's Universal Reign of Peace	Mic 4:1–4
When the Mortal Becomes Immortal	1 Cor 15:3–8, 20–26, 51–58
The Future Glory	Rom 8:18–25
The New Heaven and the New Earth	Rev 21:1–6

They are worth reading. For they are set in the overall

realities of possessions and poverty, selected by the writer of *Rich Christians in a world of hunger*, chosen by someone who has chosen to live with his family in the inner-city of Philadelphia – but can still hold to the deep-set belief that God will ultimately rule in shalom over the whole earth, that individual believers at death will 'rest in shalom', that the world to be is far greater than we can ever comprehend, and that there will be restoration and a new creation in heaven and upon earth.

For creation in Genesis and the new creation in Jesus is the establishment of shalom in a universe that apart from God's rule is chaotic, disordered, unproductive and unfulfilling.

Living in the In-between

But we live in the in-between. In his book *Christ and Time* Oscar Cullmann likens this time-zone to the span between V-Day and D-Day in the 1939–1945 war. I was then a teenager and recall the experience.

I remember D-Day. We woke up to the news about the invasion of Europe. It was 6th June 1944. This day opened the final chapter in the war. I was in London for V-E Day, 1945. We went to Trafalgar Square to join in the crowds and singing, the lights and laughter. The war was over. Peace had come.

But we had to live through the long, hurtful year in-between. There was a bitter struggle, a lot of suffering and times of despair before victory finally came.

We are living in the in-between now. D-Day dawned for Christians with the coming of Jesus. That was the invasion of the world of time by the kingdom of God. But that kingdom has not fully and finally come.

V-Day has yet to be. The battle is still on. It is going on all around us – and within us.

Don't minimise the forces of evil. They are real and powerful. The Bible calls them 'principalities and powers'. Evil has many faces and is far more than personal sin. It taints the structures and systems of our society. It is like a malevolent, creeping tide of darkness penetrating and undermining.

I grow increasingly aware of the struggles between the kingdom of light and the kingdom of darkness – and I believe the inner city is one of the central battlefields. Unemployment, racism, injustice and poverty are claiming their casualties now. The fight is on.

The conflict is real. Progress is painfully slow. Often we feel overwhelmed and sometimes taste despair.

But V-Day will come. The rule of God will be . . .

For yours is the kingdom, the power, and the glory, for ever and ever. Amen.

The shalom that Christ has offered us, then, is a whole, new, perfect and complete way of life, made known to us in our personal experience and in our communal life alike, made known to us *here and now* within the Covenant People that is his Church, yet valid through its essential reality for the whole of God's great creation, and so also for the world to come. The framework or scaffolding of that shalom God has given to us through the hand of Moses in the Law. The *end* of that shalom, however, God has given to us in the person of his only Son our Lord.[4]

G. A. F. Knight

13

Farewell

Such welcome, such farewell
                                    An old English proverb

Go in peace
                                    The Bible farewell

Profoundly Personal

Farewell is the somewhat old-fashioned word that reverses wel-fare. At its heart it is a wanting the well-being, and praying for the very best. It is a parting, final, lasting word.

Shalom is often translated as 'farewell' or is used in the separating but linking words that bridge over endings and beginnings. Since this is the closing chapter of a book entitled *Shalom, My Friends* the word of leavetaking and well-wishing is appropriate and apt.

Christian services usually close with the blessing or benediction. Two of the best-known include shalom:

May the Lord bless you and take care of you;
May the Lord be kind and gracious to you;
May the Lord look on you with favour
and give you **peace**. (Num 6:24–26)

God's **peace**, which is far beyond human understanding, will keep your hearts and minds safe in union with Christ Jesus. (Phil 4:7)

In both cases the words, whether used as a conclusion to a

Sunday service, at a funeral, in a marriage, the blessing of a child or a valediction convey hopes and prayers for the individual or group. In the right sense of the word, they are a fare-well. Benedictions are not the mere liturgical ending of worship but the final impartings of shalom. They are not a postscript that tidies up and concludes but rather a gathering together of all that God wills for his people whether that is seen in personal or corporate terms.

Biblical farewells are often profoundly personal. In the books of Samuel there are four examples of individual farewells. At the close of an emotional conversation between a priest and a woman in anguish about her childlessness Eli understands Hannah's feelings of failure and desperation. Sensing her inner cry for maternal fulfilment and completion he sends her away with the words:

> Go in **peace** and may the God of Israel give you what you have asked him for. (1 Sam 1:17)

In a very different farewell between two young men Jonathan takes farewell of David as he flees from the bitter anger of Saul. Here the original words for Goodbye (God-be-with-ye) and the binding love of a covenant are put together in Jonathan's valediction:

> **God be with you.** The Lord will make sure that you and I, and your descendants and mine, will for ever keep the sacred promise we have made to each other. (1 Sam 20:42)

The man–woman relationship where 'parting is such sweet sorrow' is illustrated by David and Abigail when, in the tangle of future uncertainty, David gently uses shalom when he tells Abigail:

> Go back home and **don't worry**. (1 Sam 25:35)

The most poignant example of a shalom farewell is that of a father to a son about to betray him. As Absalom plots a rebellion against his father, David, cloaking it in a pretence of a religious pilgrimage, David responds to his request to leave with the simple answer:

Go in **peace**. (2 Sam 15:9)

In this series of human cameos farewells are taken. A woman
in distress, a friend, a lover and a son all receive a departing
shalom. No one can read them, even at this distance in time,
without some identification and feeling.

Letting people go hurts. The stronger the relationship and
the greater the love the deeper the prayer and the more painful
the parting. When a parent 'gives away' a daughter in a
wedding the joy of the day is shot through with the inner
knowledge that the beginning of marriage ties in with the
ending of parenthood. However deep the faith the funeral
prayer 'Father, into your hands I commit his/her spirit'
combines the ultimate passing over with the yearning that one
we have loved will enter into the full, eternal shalom.

Even moving house and severing neighbourhood ties
requires a farewell ritual, especially in the inner city. Because
of the needs and often declining numbers people leave urban
congregations with very mixed feelings. Some go with a sense
of disquiet and are unable to share their going openly, others
take part in a public leave taking where congregation and
individual fare-well each other in a moving act of valediction.

The 'rites of passage' that used to cover birth, marriage and
death now need to extend to include retirement, changing jobs,
moving house and family changes. For in all these the well-
being of a person or family is at stake and 'best wishes' need to
shift into blessing and prayer that wholeness will continue.

It is significant that many farewells are linked with home –
leaving home, changing houses, creating new families, 'going
home' at death. This corporate shalom runs through human
experiences.

In biblical examples a king sends an army away from the
battlefield with the farewell:

Go back home in **peace** (1 Sam 29:7)

and in another battlefield scene a prophet's concern for the
leaderless and rejected army of Israel brings him to say:

I can see the army of Israel scattered over the hills like sheep without a shepherd. And the Lord said 'These men have no leader; let them go home in **peace**.' (1 Kgs 22:17)

When Jesus is about to part company with his disciples his farewell shows understanding and re-assurance:

Peace is what I leave with you; it is my own **peace** that I give you. I do not give it as the world does (Jn 14:27)

and Paul picks up the solidarity within and from God in his closing prayer for the church in Rome.

May God, our source of **peace**, be with all of you. (Rom 15:33)

Wholeness and Healing be Yours

We want this for ourselves. We will it for all other human beings. Wholeness instead of the partial, completeness to supersede the incompleteness, healing for the hurt, forgiveness for sin and life for death. In a world increasingly concerned with wel-fare, 'age well' or 'well being' we look for a totality of mind, body and spirit.

The theme runs right through from the earliest stories in the Old Testament to our own day. Anyone who has suffered from an embarrassing and apparently incurable skin disease under-stands the journeying of Naaman to find someone who could set him free from the sense of uncleanness and impotence. After his meeting with Elisha and his recovery following immersion in the river Jordan his offer of money is refused and he is told to

Go in **peace**. (2 Kgs 5:19)

The story links together pride and forgiveness, search and dis-covery, obedience and healing, physical well-being and worship.

The same pattern appears in the New Testament. Whether it be in the personal healing of the woman who after twelve years of internal bleeding touched the cloak of Jesus and 'had the feeling inside herself that she was healed of her trouble' and, kneeling before Jesus, is told:

My daughter, your faith has made you well. Go in **peace**, and be healed of your trouble (Mk 5:34)

or in the much wider Messianic awareness of the old priest Simeon who, confronted with the infant Jesus, recognises that God's time has come and bursts into song:

> Now, Lord, you have kept your promise,
> and you may let your servant go in **peace**.
> With my own eyes I have seen your salvation
> which you have prepared in the presence of all peoples.
> A light to reveal your will to the Gentiles
> and bring glory to your people Israel. (Lk 2:29–32)

That is why the farewell at the close of letters in the early church end where they began – with the shalom of God:

> May **peace** and mercy be with them. (Gal 6:16)

> May God the Father and the Lord Jesus Christ give to all Christian brothers **peace** and love with faith. (Eph 6:23)

> May **peace** be with all of you who belong to Christ. (1 Pet 5:14)

> **Peace** be with you. (3 Jn 15)

I want to end where we began – asking you to concentrate on one word, shalom. That was the 'diving-board' from which we jumped into this exploration of the meaning and message of this key theme. Keep it before you, search it out for yourself and apply it to your living. Use the Bible Quarry to dig more deeply and to discover fresh insights.

Understand that shalom is God's greeting to creation. It is God's pattern because it is his nature. The progressive revelation of the Old Testament that accelerated in Jesus and is made real to us by the Holy Spirit opens our eyes to see who God is and unblocks our ears to hear what he says. That greeting is for you and for the whole universe. Be whole. Peace be with you.

Look below the surface of our society to catch the yearning and the dreaming that finds expression in so many forms. Hold fast to the enduring reality of shalom within the conflicts and confusions of our own day. And remember always that this is God's gift which must be rooted in us to be fully received.

Then work out the implications of shalom in every dimension of life. Let it deepen you in your personal faith, call you into a wider experience of sharing, and stretch you to the limit in your world view.

To enter more fully into the true nature of shalom you will have to reach into the foundations and you will uncover the awkward demands of justice and righteousness. These will put uncomfortable questions to you as you continue to live within the shalom covenant, working out the consequences of that double relationship. And all the time you will journey on towards the consummation that God has planned for the created order, and for you.

Those of us who have entered into this shalom and received God's gift are called to continually reach out to others and strive for shalom. So when we greet or take farewell of anyone our prayer is for their wholeness; when we enter, live in or leave a place or district our yearning is that this part of God's world will know shalom; when we become part of a human group, whether family, friendship, work, or faith centred we strive for the one-ness of shalom; when we look around our nation and see the divisions and tensions we go on in the ministry of reconciliation; and when we mentally wrestle with the tumult of this earth and the immensities of space we hold fast to the hope that the day will come when all cohere together in the unity of God's creative purpose.

The origin and the destiny of God's people is to be on the road of shalom, which is to live with joyous memories and towards greater anticipation.[1]

May the Lord Himself, who is our source of **peace**, give you **peace** at all times and in every way. The Lord be with you all. (2 Thes 3:16)

SHALOM

14

A Biblical Quarry

A quarry has to do with digging and building. The material is already there but has to be reached, removed and shaped before building can be completed.

This section of the book corresponds to the main chapters and can be used in a number of ways:

(1) By working at the material *after* reading the chapter.
(2) By digging around *before* you read the chapter.
(3) By taking it as a major exercise following the book.
(4) By dipping whenever, and wherever, you wish.

The choice is yours!

The material is set out in full and like the main chapters whenever shalom occurs the translating word is in bold typeface. The references are gathered together in this way to avoid overloading the main chapter, and to give opportunity for concentrated work. The text is from the Good News Bible but you may wish to work at another version separately, or for comparison.

Set out to uncover for yourself the richness and the message of this vivid word. Start, if you wish, at the top and begin with the obvious and the simplest. But keep digging down and back through the inter-connecting layers till you reach the core of truth.

Think of the rock from which you came, the quarry from which you were dug. (Is 51:1)

Greetings

The direct translation of shalom as a greeting occurs five times in 1 and 2 Samuel:

> They will **greet** you. (1 Sam 10:4)
> Give **greetings** . . . sends you **greetings**. (1 Sam 25:5–6)
> **greeted** them warmly. (1 Sam 30:21)
> sent his son . . . to **greet** King David. (2 Sam 8:10)
> Ahimaaz called out a **greeting** to the King. (2 Sam 18:28)

Greetings are given at several levels. There is the genuine curiosity about someone's health or well-being seen in

> **How are you**, my friend? (2 Sam 20:9)

which is watered down in the more habitual

> they asked the Levite how he was **getting on** (Judg 18:15)

and deepened in the question God puts to the people of Jerusalem:

> Who will stop long enough to ask **how you are**? (Jer 15:5)

Sometimes shalom is used as a salute word, a salutation which carries acknowledgement and respect as in:

> We are going to Jezreel **to pay our respects** (2 Kgs 10:13)

but it is also used in the much warmer, stronger welcome greeting

> You are **welcome** in my home. (Judg 19:20)

That the greeting is much wider than one individual to another is seen in the prayer:

> **Peace** be with Israel. (Ps 125:5; 128:6)

This is extended even further in the opening words of the letter 'King Darius wrote to the people of all nations, races, and languages on earth'.

> **Greetings**! I command that throughout my empire everyone should fear and respect Daniel's God. (Dan 6:25–26)

In the New Testament the depth and width of the shalom greeting (now the Greek *eirene*) is gathered up in the double 'sending out' by Jesus recorded in Matthew and Luke:

> When you go into a house say '**Peace be with you**'. (Mt 10:12)
> And whenever you go into a house first say '**Peace** be with this house'. (Lk 10:5)

The Gospel proclamation embodied in Jesus finds its fruition in the famous Easter greeting recorded three times in John:

> **Peace** be with you (Jn 20:19, 21, 26)

and is preached by the early church:

> Proclaiming the Good News of **peace** through Jesus Christ. (Acts 10:36)

The New Testament 'greeting' that takes into itself and develops the Old Testament salutation appears in almost all the Epistles mainly in one form:

> May God our Father and the Lord Jesus Christ give you grace and **peace**. (Rom 1:7; see also 1 Cor 1:3; 2 Cor 1:2; Gal 1:3; Eph 1:2; Phil 1:2; 2 Thes 1:2; 1 Tim 1:2; 2 Tim 1:2; Tit 1:4; Philem:3)

But different, and interesting, permutations occur:

> May God our Father give you grace and **peace**. (Col 1:2)
> May grace and **peace** be yours. (1 Thes 1:1)
> May grace and **peace** be yours in full measure. (1 Pet 1:2, Jude 2)
> May God the Father and Jesus Christ, the Father's Son, give us grace, mercy and **peace**; may they be ours in truth and love. (2 Jn:3)
> Grace and peace be yours from God. (Rev 1:4)

The One Dream

You will find the shalom dream of completion, wholeness and fulfilment at all human levels. It is in the hope of a child given to Hannah:

Go in **peace** and may the God of Israel give you what you have asked him for. (1 Sam 1:17)

In the sustaining vision of a future building:

From the laying of the foundation of the Lord's Temple to its **completion**, all the work had been successful. (2 Chr 8:16)

In the wider dream for a nation:

He promises **peace** to us, his own people . . . love and faithfulness will meet; righteousness and **peace** will embrace. (Ps 85:8–10)

In international harmony:
But now the Lord my God has given me **peace** on all my borders (1 Kgs 5:4)

and in the haunting hope of the exiled:

You will leave Babylon with joy:
you will be led out of the city in **peace**.
The mountains and hills will burst into singing,
and the trees will shout for joy (Is 55:12)

and the ultimate dream:

Christ came and preached the Good News of **peace** to all.(Eph 2:17)

This dream is embodied in the Old Testament 'messianic hope':

He will be called . . . 'Prince of **Peace**'. His royal power will continue to grow; his kingdom will always be at **peace** (Is 9:6–7)

which is fulfilled in the coming of Jesus who will:

guide our steps into the path of peace (Lk 1:79)

and of whom they sang:

Glory to God in the highest heaven,
and **peace** on earth to those with whom he is pleased (Lk 2:14)

and who was recognised by Simeon:

> Now, Lord, you have kept your promise,
> and you may let your servant go in **peace**. (Lk 2:29)

In him the prophetic dream finds completion:

> We hoped for **peace** and a time of healing (Jer 8:15)
> I make those **plans** and predictions come true. (Is 44:26)

All this is gathered up into two key passages that repay careful study: Psalm 122, especially verses 6–9 where shalom is used three times and translated peace; Phil 4:7–8, where Paul sandwiches his dream between two reference to 'God's peace' in verses 7 and 9.

The Double Reality

Read carefully Lk 19:37–44 noting: The excitement of the disciples about Jesus, the shalom person (19:38) and look at Lk 1:79; 2:14; 2:29. The sadness of Jesus about the failure of shalom in the city (19:41).

With this in mind go back to the use of shalom in building and commerce.

> Use true and **honest** weights. (Deut 25:15; cf. Prov 11:1)
> Any altar you build for the Lord your God must be made of **uncut** stones. (Deut 27:6; see also Ex 20:25 and Josh 8:31)

From the early, earthy roots developed the use of shalom to depict the real. In relationships, especially close friendship

> I have told you this so that you will have **peace** by being united to me. (Jn 16:33)

In the nature of God

> The Lord is **peace**. (Judg 6:24)

The negative opposition or the non-shalom takes many forms: evil, disease, disloyalty, war, fear, over-activity or stress, despair, and sin.

They **pay me back** evil for good. (Ps 35:12; cf. Ps 37:21)
My whole body is **diseased** because of my sins. (Ps 38:3)
Even my best **friend**, the one I trusted most . . . has
turned against me. (Ps 41:9)
I have lived too long with people who hate **peace**. When I
speak of **peace** they are for war. (Ps 120:6–7)
I heard a cry of terror, a cry of fear and not of **peace**. (Jer
30:5)
You will not wear yourself out, and all these people can go
home with their **disputes settled**. (Ex 18:23)
Despair is coming. You will look for **peace** and never find
it. (Ezek 7:25)
There is no **safety** for sinners. (Is 48:22; 57:21)

The struggle for shalom is everywhere.

No-one could come and go in **safety**, because there was
trouble and disorder in every land. (2 Chr 15:5)
In the courts give real justice – the kind that brings **peace**.
Do not plan ways of harming one another. (Zech 8:16–17)

And has to do with a spiritual conflict:

God does not want us to be in disorder, but in harmony
and **peace**. (1 Cor 14:33)
God, our source of **peace**, will soon crush Satan under your
feet. (Rom 16:20)

Gift of God

Shalom is linked with the presence of God:

By David: The Lord God of Israel has given **peace** to his
people. (1 Chr 23:25)
And in the famous blessing: The Lord bless you . . . and
give you **peace**. (Num 6:24–26)

This is because it is the very nature of God

Understood by Gideon: Gideon built an altar to the Lord
there and named it 'The Lord is **peace**'. (Judg 6:23–24)

Described by the Psalmist: He promises **peace** to us, his own people . . . his saving presence will remain in our land. Love and faithfulness will meet; righteousness and **peace** will embrace. (Ps 85:8)

But this gift has to be earthed. Whether it be in the land:

I will give you **peace** in your land, and you will sleep without being afraid of anyone (Lev 26:6)

or in towns:

I will heal this city and its people and restore them to health. I will show them abundant **peace** and prosperity. (Jer 33:6)

And the gift can be rejected. When this happens

No-one can live in **peace**. (Jer 12:12; see also Jer 14:19–20; 16:5; 25:36–37)

The full making known of shalom has to be in a person such as Solomon (whose name is based on shalom).

You will have a son who will rule in **peace**, because I will give him **peace** . . . His name will be Solomon because during his reign I will give Israel **peace** and security. (1 Chr 22:9)

Shalom as a gift is fully expressed in the New Testament, especially in two Gospels. Luke underlines the coming of the gift in Jesus who will

Guide our steps into the path of **peace**. (Lk 1:79)

His birth brings

Peace on earth (Lk 2:14)

and Simeon's welcome ends with:

Now, Lord, you have kept your promise, and you may let your servant go in **peace**. (Lk 2:29)

John lets Jesus speak for himself:

Peace is what I leave with you; it is my own **peace** that I give you. (Jn 14:27)

You will have **peace** by being united with me. (Jn 16:33)
Peace be with you. (Jn 20:19, 21, 26)

For it is supremely in Jesus Christ that the shalom of God is revealed. The hope of Isaiah:

I offer **peace** to all, both near and far (Is 57:19)

is echoed by Paul:

Christ himself has brought us **peace** by making Jews and Gentiles one people . . . in order to create out of the two races one new people in union with himself, in this way making **peace**. So Christ came and preached the Good News of **peace** to all (Eph 2:14–17)

and summed up in the benedictions:

God's **peace** which is far beyond human understanding, will keep your heart and mind safe in union with Christ Jesus. (Phil 4:7)
May the God of **peace** provide you with every good thing you need in order to do his will . . . (Heb 13:20)

Rooted in Us

We need to make peace:

Now, Job, make **peace** with God and stop treating him like an enemy; if you do, then he will help you. (Job 22:21)

This is expressed in the promises and vows we make:

O God, it is right for us to praise you in Zion and keep our **promises** to you (Ps 65:1)
When you make a **vow** to the Lord your God do not put off doing what you have promised; the Lord will hold you to your **vow** and it is a sin not to keep it. (Deut 23:21)

These promises are expressed in offerings of life:

When anyone offers one of his cattle as a **fellowship** offering it is to be a bull or cow without any defects. (Lev 3:1; cf. Is 19:21) and in the life of faith:

> May you, His people, always be **faithful** to the Lord our God, obeying all his laws and commands as you do today. (1 Kgs 8:61; cf. 1 Kgs 11:4)
>
> The Lord keeps close watch over the whole world, to give strength to those whose hearts are **loyal** to him. (2 Chr 16:9; cf. 2 Kgs 20:3, 2 Chr 15:17)

This is to be seen in our obedience:

> You must perform all your duties in the fear of the Lord, faithfully **obeying** him in everything you do. (2 Chr 19:9)

Shalom has to be specific, in actions springing out of attitudes.

> When you please the Lord you can **make your enemies into friends**. (Prov 16:7)
>
> A priest will stand by his throne, and they will work together in **peace** and harmony. (Zech 6:13)

This rooting is set within the covenant:

> I will make a covenant with them that guarantees their **security**. (Ezek 34:25, 37:26)
>
> My love for you will never end; I will keep for ever my **promise of peace**. (Is 54:10)

Made Personal

Shalom has to do with personal well-being:

> Find out **how she is getting on**. (Esth 2:11)
>
> They asked about each other's **health**. (Ex 18:7)
>
> Is he **well**? he asked. He is **well**, they answered. (Gen 29:6)
>
> Find out if **everything is all right** with her, her husband, and her son. (2 Kgs 4:26)

Shalom is seen at all levels.

In human love:

> My lover knows that with him I find contentment and **peace**. (Song 8:10)

In family life:

Is the young man Absalom **safe**. (2 Sam 18:29, 32)
Go and see if your brothers are **safe**. (Gen 37:14)
He asked about their father's **health** . . . How is he? Is he still alive and **well**? (Gen 43:27)
Let me go back to my relations in Egypt to see if they are still **alive**. (Ex 4:18)

In friendship (four references in one chapter):

If he says 'All right', I will be **safe**. (1 Sam 20:7; see 1 Sam 20:13, 21)
God be with you. (1 Sam 20:42)

In wider ways:

David asked Uriah if Joab and the troops were **well**. (2 Sam 11:7)
He worked for the good of his people and for the **security** of their descendants. (Esth 10:3)
Notice the good man, observe the righteous man; a **peaceful** man has descendants. (Ps 37:37)

Shalom is made personal in many ways.

It is being 'safe':

Jacob arrived **safely**. (Gen 33:18)
In those days no-one could come and go in **safety** because there was trouble and disorder in every land. (2 Chr 15:5)

It is being 'at Home':

Go back home in **peace**. (1 Sam 29:7)
If I return **safely** to my father's home, then you will be my God. (Gen 28:21)

It is being 'blessed':

Then God will come and help you and restore your household as your **reward**. (Job 8:6)
Those who are good are **rewarded** here on earth. (Prov 11:31)
They keep saying that **all will go well** with them. (Jer 23:17)

The humble will possess the land and enjoy **prosperity and peace**. (Ps 37:11)

How great is the Lord! He is pleased with the **success** of his servant. (Ps 35:27)

Success to you and those who help you! God is on your side.(1 Chr 12:18)

It is knowing fulfilment and victory:

He will **fulfil** what he has planned for me. (Job 23:14)

Until he returned **victorious**. (2 Sam 19:24)

When I come back from the **victory**. (Judg 11:31)

Shalom has the power to remove negative factors like bitterness, fear and sin:

Heal me and let me live. My bitterness will turn into **peace**. (Is 38:16)

Don't worry. **Don't be afraid**. (Gen 43:23)

God loves you, so don't let anything **worry** you or frighten you. (Dan 10:18)

Peace is what I leave with you. (Jn 14:27)

There is no **safety** for sinners. (Is 48:22, 57:21)

In the final analysis, shalom is salvation:

Now that we have been put right with God through faith, we have **peace** with God through our Lord Jesus Christ. (Rom 5:1)

Your faith has saved you; go in **peace**. (Lk 7:50)

Your faith has made you well. Go in **peace**, and be healed of your trouble. (Mk 5:34)

For Sharing

Have the salt of friendship among yourselves, and live in **peace** with one another. (Mk 9:50)

Shalom means living together in peace:

All these people can go home with their **disputes settled**. (Ex 18:23)

King Jabin of Hazor was at **peace** with Heber's family. (Judg 4:17)

We must always aim at those things that bring **peace** and that help to strengthen one another. (Rom 14:9)

Try to be at **peace** with everyone. (Heb 12:14)

This means being 'friendly':

These men are **friendly**. (Gen 34:21)

The King wants to know if you have come as a **friend**. (2 Kgs 9:18)

They hated their brother so much that they would not speak to him in a **friendly** manner. (Gen 37:4)

The king's best **friends** misled him, they overruled him. (Jer 38:22)

It is to be seen especially in the church:

Do everything possible on your part to live in **peace** with everybody. (Rom 12:18)

Live in **peace**. And the God of love and peace will be with you. (2 Cor 13:11)

Be at **peace** among yourselves. (1 Thes 5:13)

But it has to be worked out in society:

Ours is a great city, one of the most **peaceful** and loyal in Israel. (2 Sam 20:19)

Your rulers will no longer oppress you. I will make them rule with justice and **peace**. (Is 60:17)

Work for the **good** of the cities where I have made you go as prisoners. Pray to me on their behalf, because if they are **prosperous**, you will be **prosperous** too. (Jer 29:7)

And Christians are specifically called to be peacemakers:

God has called you to live in **peace**. (1 Cor 7:15)

Strive for **peace** with all your heart. (Ps 34:14)

Happy are those who work for **peace**. (Mt 5:9)

He tried to make **peace** between them. (Acts 7:26)

Goodness is the harvest that is produced from the seeds the **peace-makers** plant in **peace**. (Jas 3:18)

The sharing of shalom is seen in the nature of God:

> God is powerful; all must stand in awe of him; he keeps his heavenly kingdom in **peace**. (Job 25:1-2)
>
> God made **peace** through his Son's death on the cross and so brought back to himself all things, both on earth and in heaven. (Col 1:20)

To Be Universal

Within the nations:
Begin with Psalm 72. Read it through, noting how shalom occurs twice:

> May the land enjoy **prosperity**. (Ps 72:3)
>
> May **prosperity** last as long as the moon gives light. (Ps 72:7)

02Rulers have both a responsibility and an expectation:

> King Hezekiah understood this to mean that there would be **peace and security** during his life-time. (Is 39:8)
>
> Your wise leadership has brought us a long period of **peace**.(Acts 24:2)

And the people have a right to shalom.

> They went to Herod and asked him for **peace**. (Acts 12:20)

But judgement will follow if God's way is neglected:

> You moan and cry out in distress because the Lord in his anger has destroyed your nation and left your **peaceful** country in ruins. (Jer 25:37)

And the only way:

> You know the message he sent to the people of Israel, proclaiming the Good News of **peace** through Jesus Christ, who is Lord of all. (Acts 10:36)

Between the nations:

> But now the Lord my God has given me **peace** on all my borders. (1 Kgs 5:4)

He keeps your borders **safe**. (Ps 147:14)
The ambassadors who tried to bring about **peace** are crying bitterly. (Is 33:7)
he will send messages to ask for terms of **peace**. (Lk 14:32)

For the whole earth:

Bringing good news, the news of **peace**. (Is 52:7)
His people will live in **safety** because people all over the earth will acknowledge his greatness, and he will bring peace. (Mic 5:4–5)
Peace on earth. (Lk 2:14)
Your king will make **peace** among the nations. (Zech 9:10)
God made **peace** through his Son's death on the cross and so brought back to himself all things, both on earth and in heaven. (Col 1:20)
Christ came and preached the Good News of **peace** to all.(Eph 2:17)

Foundations

The danger of false foundations is a key prophetic theme.

'**All is well**', they say, when all is not well. (Jer 8:11)
Everyone, great and small, tries to make money dishonestly; even prophets and priests cheat the people. They act as if my people's words were only scratches. '**All is well**', they say, when all is not well. (Jer 6:13–14)
The prophets mislead my people by saying that **all is well**. All is certainly not well. (Ez 13:10, cf. v 16)
My people are deceived by prophets who promise **peace** to those who pay them, but threaten war to those who don't. (Mic 3:5)

And the note appears in the New Testament:

When people say 'Everything is **quiet and safe**', then suddenly destruction will hit them. (1 Thes 5:3)

There is a strong link between shalom and justice:

Your rulers will no longer oppress you; I will make them
rule with justice and **peace**. (Is 60:17)
Speak the truth to one another. In the courts give real
justice – the kind that brings **peace**. (Zech 8:16)
No-one is safe when you are about. Everything you do is
unjust. You follow a crooked path, and no-one who walks
that path will ever be **safe**. (Is 59:8)

And between righteousness and shalom:

Love and faithfulness will meet; righteousness and **peace**
will embrace. (Ps 85:10)
Because everyone will do what is right, there will be **peace
and security** for ever. God's people will be free from
worries and their homes **peaceful and safe**. (Is 32:17–18)
May righteousness flourish in his life-time, and may
prosperity last as long as the moon gives light. (Ps 72:7)

God's Kingdom holds them all together:

God's Kingdom is not a matter of eating and drinking,
but of the righteousness, **peace**, and joy which the Holy
Spirit gives. (Rom 14:17; see Mt 6:33)

That kingdom is embodied in the King Jesus:

For Christ Himself has brought us **peace** by making Jew
and Gentile one people . . . To create out of the two races
one new people in union with Himself, in this way making
peace . . . So Christ came and preached the Good News
of **peace** to all. (Eph 2:14–18)

We enter into shalom and build on the right foundations
through our faith in him:

Now that we have been put right with God through faith,
we have **peace** with God through our Lord Jesus Christ.
(Rom 5:1)
May grace and **peace** be yours in full measure through
your knowledge of God and of Jesus our Lord. (2 Pet 1:2)

Continuation

The idea of a continuing shalom is seen in the use of 'guarantees'.

> David gave Abner a **guarantee of safety.** (2 Sam 3:21; repeated in vv 22 and 23)

This is lifted into the covenant:

> I will make a covenant with them that **guarantees their security** (Ezek 34:25; see 37:26)

with its human side of promise:

> Let me go . . . and keep a **promise** (2 Sam 15:7)

and the Godward, eternal, aspect:

> I will keep for ever my promise of **peace**. (Is 54:10)

This is picked up in the metaphor of a path:

> To guide our steps into the path of **peace**. (Lk 1:79; cf. Is 59:8)
> They have not known the path of **peace**. (Rom 3:17)

Which is completed in the one-ness with the one who is the way through our faith:

> I have told you this so that you will have **peace** by being united to me. (Jn 16:33)
> May God, the source of hope, fill you with all joy and **peace** by means of your faith in him. (Rom 15:13)

This is worked out by the way we live in shalom:

> Do everything possible on your part to live in **peace** with everybody. (Rom 12:18)
> Live in **peace**. And the God of love and **peace** will be with you. (2 Cor 13:11)

In this there will be effort or striving:

> Turn away from evil and do good. Strive for **peace** with all your heart. (Ps 34:14 quoted in 1 Pet 3:11)
> Strive for righteousness, faith, love and **peace**. (2 Tim 2:22)

This is to be worked out in detail, e.g., in marriage.

> God has called you to live in **peace**. (1 Cor 7:15)

But continuation is not possible without 'the wisdom from above':

> The wisdom from above is pure first of all . . . it is also **peaceful**, gentle, and friendly, it is full of compassion and produces a harvest of good deeds; it is free from prejudice and hypocrisy. And goodness is the harvest that is produced from the seeds the **peacemakers** plant in **peace**. (Jas 3:17–18).

And this is made possible by the gift of the Holy Spirit:

> To be controlled by the Spirit results in life and **peace**. (Rom 8:6)
> The Spirit produces . . . **peace** . . . (Gal 5:22)
> Do your best to preserve the unity which the Spirit gives by means of the **peace** that binds you together. (Eph 4:3)

This wisdom and the Spirit enables us to continue to work at shalom as peacemakers, in worship, in fellowship and in proclamation:

> Happy are those who work for **peace**. God will call them His children. (Mt 5:9)
> God does not want us to be in disorder but in harmony and **peace**. (1 Cor 14:33)
> The **peace** that Christ gives is to guide you in the decisions you make; for it is to this **peace** that God has called you together in the one body. (Col 3:15)
> The readiness to announce the Good News of **peace**. (Eph 6:15)

Consummation

Shalom means 'finished' in the completion of a task.

> The temple is still not **finished**. (Ezra 5:16)

After fifty two days of work the entire wall was **finished**. (Neh 6:15)

Shalom means 'all' in the total, numerical sense:

All the people of Judah have been taken away into exile. (Jer 13:19)
They carried off a **whole** nation and sold them as slaves.(Amos 1:6)

The theme is notable in the building of the Temple in which shalom is used for preparation (going towards) and completion.

The stones with which the temple was built **had been prepared** at the quarry. (1 Kgs 6:7)
When King Solomon **finished** all the work on the temple. (1 Kgs 7:51; cf. 1 Kgs 9:25)
By this time all Solomon's projects had been completed. From the laying of the foundation of the Lord's Temple to its **completion**, all the work had been successful. (2 Chr 8:16)

In personal life shalom becomes the harvest or reward:

Those who have been disciplined by such punishment reap the **peaceful** reward of a righteous life. (Heb 12:11)

This is strongly so in the consummation of death:

You yourself will live to a ripe old age, die in **peace**, and be buried. (Gen 15:15)
Those who live good lives will find **peace** and rest in death. (Is 57:2)
You will die in **peace**. (Jer 34:5)
(See also 1 Kgs 2:6, 2 Kgs 22:20, 2 Chr 34:28, Is 38:12, 60:20)

The New Testament resurrection and Easter Day focus in Jesus:

Peace be with you. (Jn 20:19, 21, 26)

But shalom as consummation is much greater than the personal:

I make those plans and predictions **come true**. (Is 44:26)
God has numbered the days of your kingdom and brought
it to an **end**. (Dan 5:26)
God, our source of **peace**, will soon crush Satan under your
feet. (Rom 16:20)
And so, my friends, as you wait for that Day, do your best
to be pure and faultless in God's sight and to be at **peace**
with him. (2 Pet 3:14)
(See also 1 Thes 5:23 and Heb 13:20)

Farewell

The last word is shalom:

May the Lord bless you and take care of you;
May the Lord be kind and gracious to you;
May the Lord look on you with favour;
and give you **peace**. (Num 6:24–26)
God's **peace**, which is far beyond human understanding,
will keep your hearts and minds safe in union with Christ
Jesus. (Phil 4:7)

Shalom in farewells. To a woman in distress:

Go in **peace** and may the God of Israel give you what you
have asked him for. (1 Sam 1:17)

Between friends:

God be with you. The Lord will make sure that you and I,
and your descendants and mine, will for ever keep the
sacred promise we have made to each other. (1 Sam 20:42)

Between lovers:

Go back home and don't worry. (1 Sam 25:35)

A father to a son:

Go in **peace**. (2 Sam 15:9)

Shalom means 'going home'. A king sends an army back:

Go back home in **peace**. (1 Sam 29:7)

A prophet asks that another army return.

I can see the army of Israel scattered over the hills like sheep without a shepherd. And the Lord said 'These men have no leader; let them go home in **peace**'. (1 Kgs 22:17)

In the New Testament Jesus gives a new dimension to farewell:

Peace is what I leave with you; it is my own **peace** that I give you. I do not give it as the world does (Jn 14:27)

and Paul echoes this:

May God, the source of **peace**, be with all of you. (Rom 15:33)

Shalom-farewell wishes wholeness and healing:

Go in **peace**. (2 Kgs 5:19)
My daughter your faith has made you well. Go in **peace**, and be healed of your trouble. (Mk 5:34)

But is much wider than the personal:

Now, Lord, you have kept your promise,
and you may let your servant go in **peace**.
With my own eyes I have seen your salvation
which you have prepared in the presence of all peoples.
A light to reveal your will to the Gentiles
and bring glory to your people Israel. (Lk 2:29–32)

Personal and corporate shalom are drawn together in the New Testament farewells:

May **peace** and mercy be with them. (Gal 6:16)
May God the Father and the Lord Jesus Christ give to all Christian brothers **peace** and love with faith. (Eph 6:23)
May God our Father and the Lord Jesus Christ give you grace and **peace**. (Phil 1:2)
May **peace** be with all of you who belong to Christ. (1 Pet 5:14)
Peace be with you. (3 Jn 15)

15

Contemporary Workshop

*Strive for **peace** with all your heart.*
Psalm 34:14, quoted in 1 Peter 3:11

Shalom has to be worked at. We are called to be peacemakers in our own day. That means we are in a contemporary workshop. Shalom has to be made real and relevant now. In a variety of ways and at many levels we work towards shalom.

This book is open-ended. You are now to go out and to go on. Wherever you are and whatever you do shalom is on your agenda. All around you others are already into shalom-ministry. Your task is to learn from them or to work with them.

This chapter gives you some pointers and indicates where resources are available.

Begin where you are

Look around you. Discover what is already going on in your own church and community.

● In your congregation – search out those actively engaged in striving for shalom. Ask your leaders and talk it over with your friends. There's pastoral care, evangelism and social action. It may be family centred or work with the elderly; it could be youth work or counselling.
● In your community – discover what is going on and who is doing it. Read your local paper, listen to the radio and find those with knowledge of your neighbourhood. What are the

unmet needs, the hidden hurts and the signs of hope? Your local council for Social Services links together the voluntary agencies – ask for their directory or talk to their workers to find out what is going on. Go into your Town Hall, contact your Councillor, ask to see your MP – they'll be surprised and pleased to meet you. Find out what other Christians are doing – operating a housing association, sharing in a visiting scheme, facing social issues?

● In your work – look around at the individuals and the structures. Who do you relate to? Where are the points of communication or unity? Think through how wholeness and harmony can be achieved. That could mean active membership of a trade union or a fresh look at management skills.

Team up with others

Shalom is corporate and must be worked out in a togetherness.

● Be part of a task-force. Build together a group of people determined to tackle one specific task. It could be raising awareness of the peace agenda, tackling a particular environmental or ecological issue or launching a new-style bridge project for evangelism.

● Look out for others already working. Co-operation is better than competition, consultation will prevent imposition, collaboration cuts out dependency. So check out the yellow-pages, contact one of the co-ordinating bodies, phone your local paper or write to your area or neighbourhood councils – political as well as church!

● Work with, and not for, people. In evangelism, build bridges and create relationships rather than scatter tracts. In social care, create self-help groups rather than imposed programmes. Go to the people, live among them, learn from them, love them, serve them and plan with them. Start with what they know and build with what they have. Learn by doing and teach by living.

Explore the possibilities

● Down your street. That could be sharing in 'Neighbourhood Watch' or starting a house group; it might mean visiting or creating a community life. You can get the names from the electoral roll, ideas from your postman or milkman and encouragement from the unlikely.

● In your area. Learn the art of networking, join hands with others who share your concern, celebrate the faith across the lines. That could be unemployment (start a job-shop) or politics (does anyone pray with politicans?) or a multi-faith group (do you really know what the Muslims believe?) or an act of witness (united carols in the Town Hall!).

● Across the nation. If you are in a church your denomination will have a social responsibility department – write to find out what they're tackling. Single-parents, alcoholism, Aids, students, racism . . . ? On a wider basis watch out for groups emphasising a key-theme. The UK Christian Handbook available from Marc Europe, Cosmos House, 6 Homesdale Road, Bromley, Kent BR2 9EX at £12.95 has pages of national groups already at work and your own church newspaper carries advertisements giving details and addresses.

Do be definite

In putting together your own abilities, other needs and the purpose of God you will need to be single-minded. Select a key issue, gather information and decide how to act. Here are some examples:

Poverty

Get facts and figures, programmes and policies from the Child Poverty Action Group, 4th floor, 1/5 Bath Street, London, EC1V 9PY.

Discover Christian approaches and networks from Church Action on Poverty, Central Buildings, Oldham Street, Manchester, M1 1JT (Tel: 061-236-9321). Projects and experiments can be found in Methodism's Mission Alongside the Poor, 1 Central Buildings, Westminster, London, SW1H 9NU.

Race issues

Write for the JCG Bulletin from the Community and Race Relations Unit, British Council of Churches, 2 Eaton Gate, London, SW1W 9BL. Contact the Evangelical Christians for Racial Justice at 12 Bell Barn Shopping Centre, Birmingham 15 2DZ (Tel: 021-622-6807), or find out what the ZEBRA Project does – 1 Merchant Street, London, E3 4LY.

Unemployment

Church Action with the Unemployed, Holywell Centre, 1 Phipp Street, London, EC2A 4PS (Tel: 01-729-1434) has good introductory leaflets. Evangelical Enterprises at the Evangelical Alliance, 186, Kennington Park Road, London, SE11 4BT is a new, networking, locally rooted initiative.

Families

Ask your national church for literature and groups or get in touch with The Families Adviser, Scripture Union House, 130 City Road, London, EC1V 2NJ (Tel: 01-250-1966), or Familybase, Jubilee Centre, 3 Hooper Street, Cambridge CB1 2NZ (Tel: 0223-311596).

Church unity

If you want to know more about the Inter-Church Process get details from the B.C.C., 2 Eaton Gate, London, SW1W 9BL or the Catholic Truth Society, 38/40 Eccleston Square, London, SW1V 1PD. Locally you can join in the special Lent groups, the Week of Prayer for Christian Unity or (best of all) gather together neighbouring Christians.

Money

Consider seriously how you use your money. Apply shalom principles to your giving – church, special issues, world concerns. Make sure your will reflects your interests! Look hard at the use of covenants, whether directly or through the Charities Aid Foundation.

If you are investing money think about ethical investments. The Ethical Investment and Research Information Services, 9 Poland Street, London W1 (Tel: 01-439-2771) can give you an overview and at least four funds are already operating:

Stewardship Trust – Managed by Friends' Provident
Fellowship Trust – Buckmaster
Ethical Trust – Abbey Life
Conscience Fund – N. M. Schroder

Community life

The community movement finds expression in a diversity of styles. The National Association of Christian Centres and Networks, Westhill College, Weoley Park Road, Birmingham, B29 6LL (Tel: 021-472-8079) publishes the magazine *Community*. *Body Book* is a directory of fellowships 'moving in renewal or restoration' compiled by Team Spirit and available from P.O. Box 16, Romford, Essex, RM5 3TN.

The world

Get materials from One World Week, P.O. Box 100, London, SE1 7RT (Tel: 01-620-4444). This is backed by many churches, missionary societies and agencies. The intention is to bring the Gospel call for justice and peace to the centre of church life.

You can follow through at several levels. The World Development Movement, Bedford Chambers, Covent Garden, London, WC2E 8HA has regional representatives. Christian Aid, Tear Fund and CAFOD tackle relief. Friends of the Earth and Greenpeace are into environmental issues. Amnesty concentrates on prisoners of conscience. Missionary societies cover a wide range of shalom-ministry, write to them for information.

Urban mission

Several networks now draw together inner city and urban poor ministries. The Evangelical Coalition for Urban Mission, 130 City Road, London, EC1V 2NJ (Tel: 01-250-1966) links together four organisations concerned with evangelism, youth work, race issues and research and Christian Organisations for Social, Political and Economic Change (COSPEC) c/o 18 Rattray Road, London, SW2 is a federation of groups committed to the struggle for a just, participatory and sustainable society. Centre Point, St John's Parish Office, 18 Larcom Street, London, SE17 1BR offers residential opportunity for people to get into contact with inner city life while the Urban Theology Unit, Pitsmoor Study House, 210 Abbeyfield Road, Sheffield, S4 7AZ (Tel: 0742-388035) is a well-established training programme with projects and publications. Anglicans and Methodists have their own specific thrusts through Faith in the City and Mission Alongside the Poor (MAP).

Goodness is the harvest that is produced from the seeds the peace-makers plant in shalom

James 3:18

References

Chapter 1

1. Roger Dowley, *Towards the Recovery of a Lost Bequest*, (A layman's work notes on the biblical pattern for a just community). Evangelical Coalition for Urban Mission, 1984.
2. Walter Brueggemann, *Living Toward a Vision*. Biblical reflections on shalom. United Church Press (USA), 1976.
3. Perry B. Yoder, *Shalom: The Bible's Word for Salvation, Justice, and Peace.* Faith and Life Press (USA), 1987.
4. Walter Brueggemann, op. cit. p. 53.
5. Perry B. Yoder, op. cit. p. 8.
6. Roger Dowley, op. cit. p. 36.
7. Bruce Dutton writing in *Green Shoots in the Concrete*, p. 168. Towards a more sensitive Christian presence in our cities. Peter Kaldor (Australia), 1985.

Chapter 2

1. Gerhard Kittell, *Theological Dictionary of the New Testament*, Vol II, p. 402, Eerdmans, 1964.
2. *The Alternative Service Book*, The Church of England, 1980.
3. Johannes B. Baver (Editor), *Encyclopaedia of Biblical Theology*, Vol II, p. 648, Sheed and Ward, 1970.

Chapter 3

1. Walter Brueggemann. op. cit. p. 5.
2. Bruce Chatwin, *The Song Lines*, Cape, 1987.
3. *The Guardian*, 17.8.87.
4. Margaret Drabble, *Jerusalem the Golden*, p. 35, Weidenfeld & Nicolson, 1967.
5. George Eugeniou, *The Earthians*. A poem.

Chapter 4

1. T. S. Eliot, *Burnt Norton*.
2. Philip Sheldrake, *Images of Holiness*, p. 12. Explorations in Contemporary Spirituality. Darton, Longman & Todd, 1987.

3. *The Guardian*, 5.12.87.
4. Walter Brueggemann. op. cit. p. 20.
5. Hugh Thomas, 'The Kingdom is Here', *NOW* magazine, May 1984.

Chapter 5

1. H. Beck, C. Brown, Article on peace, *The New International Dictionary of New Testament Theology*, Vol 2, p. 777, Paternoster, 1976.
2. Dwight L. Moodey.
3. Jim Punton, *What hope for shalom?* B.C.C., 1975.
4. Perry B. Yoder. op. cit. p. 21.
5. Jim Punton. op. cit.

Chapter 6

1. From Prayers produced by the House of the Gentle Bunyip, Melbourne.
2. Colin Marchant (Editor), *Christian Outreach to the Urban Poor*, Lausanne, 1980.
3. Martin Wallace, *Healing Encounters in the City*. Insights from an urban perspective. Grove Pastoral Series, No. 30, p. 3.
4. George A. F. Knight, *A Christian Theology of the Old Testament*, p. 250, S.C.M., 1959.

Chapter 7

1. Alan Kreider, *Journey towards Holiness*, p. 99, Marshall Pickering, 1986.
2. Perry B. Yoder op. cit. p. 12.
3. *An Evangelical Commitment to Simple Life-style*, Lausanne Occasional Paper No. 20, p. 17, 1980.
4. Richard Foster, *Money, Sex, and Power*, p. 86, Hodder & Stoughton, 1985.
5. Joint Christian Group on Race Relations Bulletin, Churches Information on Racial Justice, Vol 2, No 2, January 1987.
6. *The Observer*, 27.12.87.
7. Ibid.

Chapter 8

1. Richard Foster, *Freedom of Simplicity*, p. 30, Triangle/SPCK, 1981.
2. Kittell, op. cit. p. 406.
3. *New International Dictionary of New Testament Theology*, op. cit. p. 777.
4. Perry B. Yoder, op. cit. p.13.
5. John Stott, *Issues facing Christians today*, p. 101–2, Marshalls, 1984.
6. J.C.G.R.R. op. cit.

Chapter 9

1. John V. Taylor, *Enough is enough*, p. 59, S.C.M. Press, 1975.
2. Walter Brueggemann, op. cit. p. 123.
3. *Faith in the City*. A Call for Action by Church and Nation. The Report of the Archbishop of Canterbury's Commission on Urban Priority Areas, Church House Publishing, 1985.
4. Perry B. Yoder, op. cit. p. 114.

Chapter 10

1. Waldron Scott, *Bring Forth Justice*. A Contemporary Perspective on Mission. Marshalls, 1980.
2. Evangelical Coalition for Urban Mission, 130 City Road, London, EC1.
3. Perry B. Yoder, op. cit. p. 5.
4. Kenneth Leech, *True God*, p. 379, Sheldon Press, 1985.

Chapter 11

1. John F. Kennedy, in an address to the UN Assembly, 20.9.63.
2. Kittell, op. cit. p. 403.
3. A. H. Dammers, *Life Style. A parable of sharing*, p. 9, Turnstone Press, 1982.
4. *An Evangelical Commitment to Simple Life Style*, op. cit. p. 30.
5. Howard Snyder, *Liberating the Church*, The Ecology of Church and Kingdom, p. 11, Marshalls, 1983.
6. *The Guardian*, 24.4.87.

Chapter 12

1. *New International Dictionary of New Testament Theology*, op. cit. p. 778.
2. Walter Brueggemann, op. cit. p. 74.
3. Ronald Sider, *Cry Justice*. The Bible speaks on hunger and poverty. Paulist Press, 1980.
4. G. A. F. Knight, *Law and Grace*, p. 89, S.C.M. Press, 1962.

Chapter 13

1. Walter Brueggemann, op. cit. p. 16.

ISSUES FACING CHRISTIANS TODAY

John Stott

A major appraisal of contemporary social, moral, sexual and global issues, combined with one man's attempt to think 'Christianly' on this broad spectrum of complex questions, make ISSUES FACING CHRISTIANS TODAY a *best-seller*.

'This is powerful stuff. Highly contemporary . . . awkwardly personal . . . thoroughly biblical.'   *Baptist Times*

'A valuable resource for Christians responding to the huge needs to seek the renewal of society.'   *Buzz*

'It stands alone as a scholarly, scriptural and profoundly well-argued and researched authority on many of the most perplexing and intractable problems of the present day.'   *Renewal*

THE INFINITE GUARANTEE: A Meditation on the Last Words from the Cross

Andrew Cruickshank

A profound and thoughtful series of reflections on Jesus' seven sayings from the Cross by one of TV's most familiar and favourite actors. Andrew Cruickshank's deeply challenging study provides ideal devotional reading material, which encourages us to establish their significance of Jesus' words for us today.

'. . . a very remarkable book . . . quite outstanding. It demands to be read, re-read and read again. I can only describe it as *a little masterpiece . . .*'   Rev Dr William Neil

TWO MILLION SILENT KILLINGS: the Truth about Abortion

Dr Margaret White

Essential, informed reading for all Christians on this critical contemporary issue; likely to engender wholehearted and healthy controversy.

GP Margaret White exposes the deliberate attempt to confuse the public over the issue of abortion by the use of euphemistic language and the minimizing of its harmful side-effects. She traces the history of abortion from legal, medical and religious perspectives, describes the clinical methods used to terminate pregnancies, and answers the various arguments put forward by the pro-abortionists in terms of God's basic rules for life. At the heart of these is the Creator's desire for his creation's health, stability and well-being. Dr White demonstrates that the extent of the damaging effects of abortion on women and society is one of today's best-kept secrets.

THE GOSPEL COMMUNITY

John Tiller

An important and timely call to the established churches to rediscover the distinctive life of the Spirit and to become true 'gospel communities' – attractive, authoritative and relevant.

Neither the experience of renewal nor nationwide evangelistic missions resulted in a mass return to the churches. Instead, the house church seems to promise a better future for Christianity. Can revival still come through the established churches? John Tiller, Chancellor and Canon Residentiary of Hereford Cathedral, looks at Jesus' radical definitions of the temple, priesthood and sacrifice, and outlines the style of leadership which will enable the church to become again a 'living temple'. A critical book practically showing the way ahead for the established church.

If you wish to receive *regular information* about *new books*, please send your name and address to:

London Bible Warehouse
PO Box 123
Basingstoke
Hants RG23 7NL

Name...

Address ....

....

....

....

I am especially interested in:
☐ **Biographies**
☐ **Fiction**
☐ **Christian living**
☐ **Issue related books**
☐ **Academic books**
☐ **Bible study aids**
☐ **Children's books**
☐ **Music**
☐ **Other subjects**